~Histor

M000211379

Why We Shouldn't Call Our Ancestors Slaves

LaRue Nedd, BLD

FNNC Publishing **3rd Edition**

Why We Shouldn't Call Our Ancestors Slaves

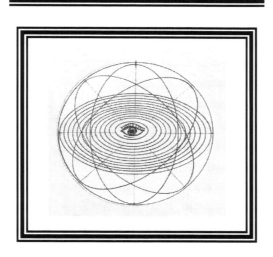

Why We Shouldn't Call Our Ancestors Slaves

3rd Edition, Revised 2012

Copyright © 1993, 2009, 2012 by (LaRue Nedd, BLD)

Published by FNNC Publishing

ISBN-10: (0985689609)

ISBN-13: (978-0-9856896-0-5)

LCCN: 2012953343

Cover Photo by Cheryl Franklin

The Impossible Dream

(Written by Mitch Leigh & Joe Darion)

To dream the impossible dream,

To fight the unbeatable foe,

To bear with unbearable sorrow,

To run where the brave dare not go

To right the unrightable wrong,

To love pure and chaste from afar,

To try when your arms are too weary,

To reach the unreachable star.

This is my quest,

To follow that star

No matter how hopeless,

No matter how far.

To fight for the right

Without question or pause,

To be willing to march Into hell for a heavenly cause.

And I know if I'll only be true to this glorious quest

That my heart will be peaceful and calm when I'm laid
   to my rest.

And, the world will be better for this,

That, one man (or woman) scorned and covered with
   scars still strove with his last ounce of courage.

To reach the unreachable star.

To dream the impossible dream

To fight the unbeatable foe

To bear with unbearable sorrow

To run where the brave dare not go.

To right the unrightable wrong

To be better far than you are

To try when your arms are too weary

To reach the unreachable star.

This is my quest, to follow that star,

No matter how hopeless, no matter how far

To be willing to give when there's no more to give

To be willing to die so that honor and justice may live

And I know if I'll only be true to this glorious quest

That my heart will lie peaceful and calm when I'm laid
   to my rest.

They set the slave free, striking off his chains...

Then he was as much of a slave as ever...

His slavery was not in his chains, but in himself...

They can only set free men free...

And there is no need of that:

Free men set themselves free.

--James Oppenheim

We are freeing ourselves in the past from the present.

We are either part of the solution or part of the problem.

When people ask me how many children do I have,

I say:

"All of them."

CONTENTS

INTRODUCTION

The aphorism, "as a man thinketh in his heart so is he," not only embraces the whole of a man's being, but is so comprehensive as to reach out to every condition and circumstance of his life. A man is literally what he thinks, his character being the complete sum of all his thoughts...

As the plant springs from, and could not be without, the seed, so every act of a man springs from the hidden seeds of thought, and could not have appeared without them. This applies equally to those acts called "spontaneous" and "unpremeditated" as to those which are deliberately executed.[1]

> --James Allen
> As A Man Thinketh

In the end, all that any of us want to do is to live and enjoy life. If we have children, we want to see them do the same thing. Sometimes, we automatically feel good when we can help other people. According to our expressions through music, art, and writing, it seems that most of us are living in hell on Earth instead of heaven on Earth. If you judge a tree by the fruit it produces, it does not look like the Black African American people are a happy people; and

Why We Shouldn't Call Our Ancestors Slaves

according to the statistics and what we can see, it shows in every area of our society.

The question is; Do Black people need self-help books specifically written for the African American? One of the reasons why most self-help books fail Black people is that they do not get to the root of the problem. They do not take our history, our environment, and our situation as a people into consideration. They analyze and diagnose our problems as if the effects of slavery have dissipated. However, the fact is that many of the changes that were imposed on us, as a people, during slavery are still with us to this day.

They act as if Black people's problems and White people's problems are the same and work the same way because we are all human beings. Although there are similarities, there are also differences. There are differences in our genetics, our spirituality, and our histories. Therefore, the dynamics of our problems are not the same as they are for White people.

One difference is obvious. When you look at the problems in American society, in every area, we suffer more. The Foster Childcare System is full of our children. Heinous and nonsensical crimes, shootings and homicide rates are epidemic in Black communities across America. We see high rates of alcohol, drug and sexual abuse.

INTRODUCTION

And, although it is not considered to be a crime, **the most devastating problem** that Black people face is the **division that exists in our families.** In fact, there is so much division in our families and communities that we now see it as being normal. One parent cannot do what two parents can do. Two parents cannot do what an extended family can do. When grandma and grandpa are not present, much knowledge and wisdom is lost. The breakup and dysfunction of our families tends to stunt the mental and spiritual growth of our children and prevents them from being competitive with others who come from healthy functional families.

These problems are not restricted to poor Black people. As adults, one way or another, the vast majority of us are caught-up in a battle for self-control. Too many of us are in a self-destruct mode and not understanding why. The aim of this book is to help improve the quality of life for Black people by providing information that will help improve the way we see ourselves which will automatically influence the way we act toward each other.

Every since we were brought here to be "slaves", which was not that long ago, the status and mental condition of Black people have always been in question even by Black people. Therefore, in the introduction of Tom Burrell's book, *Brainwashed,* he asks:

Why We Shouldn't Call Our Ancestors Slaves

So then why, after all this time, when calculating the achievement of the "American Dream," are we still ranked at the bottom of almost every "good" list, and at the top of the "bad" lists? Why, despite our apparent strength, intelligence, and resourcefulness, do we continue to lag behind and languish in so many aspects of American life?[2]

The subtitle of his books is, *"Challenging the Myth of Black Inferiority."* And, that is exactly what this book is doing as well. All myths about Black inferiority are rooted in the idea that our ancestors were slaves to the Europeans and that we lived like savages in Africa before we were brought here.

If you were kidnapped at a young age and put in an environment where everyone including the church, the school, and the news media told you that you were inferior; after a time, you would begin to believe it. The belief that Black people are inferior is the legacy of slavery.

We may not admit it openly, but many of us believe it. The proof shows in our standards of beauty, our words and our actions as a people. If we look closely at the pandemic problems that exist amongst us as a people, it would not be difficult to see that these problems are related

INTRODUCTION

to self-esteem issues. They are directly related to how we view and value ourselves as a people.

Some of us have even been convinced that something is intrinsically wrong with Black people. They believe that we are inferior by Nature or GOD's will and that slavery took us out of savagery. They also believe that Euro-American culture and religion are universally correct. They reject their African identity and culture. Therefore, the only reason they call themselves Black or African American is because they have no choice.

Believing that our ancestors were slaves has an effect on our perception of who we are and what we do. If we believe that our ancestors were slaves, then we must also believe that we are the descendants of slaves. And, in believing so, we will act accordingly. One major theme of this book is that we act according to what we think we are.

I am not saying that **"slavery"** did not exist. I am saying that the word **slave** does not and should not be applied to the ancestors of Black African Americans or any Black African people. Some people believe that if we did not call them slaves it would diminish our understanding of slavery and its impact. In truth, our understanding of our history is further diminished by calling our ancestors slaves because it tends to move us to not look at our history by not studying it and not thinking about it. It prompts us to avoid studying our history from our point of view.

Why We Shouldn't Call Our Ancestors Slaves

Many books have been written and documentaries made, and still are being made, about the various aspects of slavery. Slavery is probably **the most written about subjects in American history**. In addition, slavery has had the greatest influence on African people in modern times. Therefore, it deserves our attention. However, the more we look at the effect of calling and believing that our ancestors were slaves the more we will see the importance of this issue.

Although some of us have rejected the idea that our ancestors were slaves, understanding the reasons and the effects of calling them slaves needs to be explored. Does calling our ancestors slaves have an effect on our self-concept? Does it affect our ability to think clearly and logically? Does it affect our ability to prosper in an environment that has a long history of oppressing Black people?

Every self-help book ever written, including the Bible, tells us that there is a direct relationship between our thoughts, beliefs, actions and the results we get. Therefore, how do our thoughts about our origins, our ancestry and our history affect us?

Many social programs, books and speeches have sought to raise the consciousness and quality of life for Black people. Still, the disparity widens because we have not gotten to the root of the problem. The success rates of these programs would be much higher if we had a more positive understanding of where we came from, our true Spirit and Nature, and our situation.

This is true because we act on what we see; and, what we see is influenced, filtered and colored by what we believe about ourselves. And, our beliefs about our identity are central to what we do and the results we get. There is a connection between what a person thinks or does not think about their race and what they think about their self as a member of that race or group of people.

In examining the problems that plague Black communities across this country, we can see that the majority of our problems are related to our self-concept, our ego and our self-esteem, which is rooted in our beliefs and perception of Black people.

All are Effected

All Black people, rich and poor, are in the same American boat. Calling our ancestors slaves affects the esteem of all Black people, rich and poor, because it speaks about the quality of our nature by way of the people from whom we descended. Money does not heal these problems. In some cases, money may even make them worse because of what people must go through to get the money. Money also gives people more power to act on the negative thoughts that possess them.

Why We Shouldn't Call Our Ancestors Slaves

The belief that our ancestors were slaves was implanted in all of us at an early age. And, because it relates to the people from whom we descended, it is impossible for this belief to not have an effect on all Black African Americans.

From the Black African American activist to those who are well educated in African culture and customs to those who know nothing about African or African American history, all have been affected by the belief that our Ancestors were slaves. If you believe it, you are directly affected. If you do not believe it, you are indirectly affected by the people you know that do believe it. If it has an effect on our children, it has an effect on us. Therefore, there are no Black people who have not been affected by the belief that their ancestors were slaves.

All of us know that there is nothing good or positive about being a slave or being called a slave especially in the context of American and European history. Many of us think that we must accept this belief because it is true. Therefore, it is important that we examine the truthfulness and the effects of calling our ancestors slaves. The word "slave" is a negative word. If we apply it to our ancestors, the people from whom we descended, we also apply it to ourselves.

INTRODUCTION

The first time

Imagine how our children feel when they are bused into schools where they are the minority. Imagine them sitting in a classroom and being one of two or three Black kids out of twenty or more White children in the class. Then, imagine how they feel when they begin to learn about American history.

American history is full of examples of how Europeans came to America, conquered the land and people, and overcame all other types of adversity. They give credit for their triumphs to their spirit as a people. At the same time, our children are taught that the Black African people were slaves to the Euro-American people. At that point, what could possibly be going through our children's minds?

In the late 1950's, when I was very young, I use to get up every Saturday morning to watch Tarzan on TV. That was about the only time Black people could be seen on television. I tried to look behind Tarzan to see what the Africans were doing because they looked like me. However, they were too far in the background and all I could get was a glimpse. Still, every Saturday I hoped I would get a chance to learn a little more about Black people and my heritage.

In those days, one of the worst things a person could call you was a "black dog." The word black was more painful than the word dog. At the same time, if you told someone to do something that they did not want to do, they would respond with, **"I ain't your slave."** Being a slave was considered to be as bad as or worse than being a black dog.

In the mid 1960's, Black people were starved for positive social and cultural recognition. (And, we still are to this day.) That is why I got excited when I learned that we were going to learn about Black people's history in our Social Studies period. I was ready to learn. Then, the first thing the teacher showed us in the book was that Black people were slaves to White people. I was disappointed again. Being dark skinned was bad enough, and being the descendant of slaves seemed like a double blow to me.

Do you remember how you felt the first time you learned you were a descendant of slaves? What did you think? If you did not feel anything, it had to be because you had already been numbed by the system. Today, our children are much more aware of things than we were at their age. What are they learning about their history, their ancestors, and who they are? What are they thinking? Do they even care?

Today, the propaganda machine is even more pervasive and effective in mis-educating us about us and projecting negative images of Black people. Their messages are subtle and subliminal. Almost every Black

INTRODUCTION

African American activist recognizes that the images being projected today are only updated versions of those projected during slavery and the Jim Crow era.

If we accept these negative images as true, we will act accordingly, making what we believe come true. Then, they become self-fulfilling beliefs. As a result, these negative images cause us to suffer disproportionately in the land of plenty. Because we have been bombarded with information that says our ancestors were slaves, it is not enough just to say that our ancestors were not slaves. We must understand the logic and the effect that the word slave has on the psyche of Black people. Our children must know that their ancestors were not slaves and that they are not the descendents of slaves.

No healing can take place until the illness is acknowledged and understood.

Why We Shouldn't Call Our Ancestors Slaves

THE PRINCIPLES & ISSUES

What is in a name? Does the belief that our ancestors were slaves have an effect on our identity and self-concept? Exactly what do we mean when we call our ancestors slaves? How does this name affect us? If names have no effect, then what difference does it make what we call our ancestors or ourselves?

I think that most people believe that the names we apply to ourselves are very important. Therefore, one of the biggest debates in the Black community is over the use of the "N" word. The fact that we call it the "N word" and the debate itself implies the importance of the names we use to identify ourselves as individuals and as a people.

Principles of Thought

Since this book is about the effects of calling our ancestors slaves, it is necessary for us to examine some basic laws of how the mind works and how thoughts and beliefs work. Just like everything else in this world, **our thoughts and beliefs function according to universal laws and order**. Universal laws do not change and cannot be changed. Under specific conditions, they will produce specific results every time.

Why We Shouldn't Call Our Ancestors Slaves

Every thought and belief that we have has an **avenue, a cause and an effect**. Thoughts and ideas also contain qualities that can be compared to living things such as plants or animals. They struggle and compete to exist in the conscious mind. They require energy to survive. In addition, they can remain active in the mind even though we may not be aware of them.

We have a symbiotic relationship with our thoughts and beliefs. We feel that they are a vital part of us. If our thoughts and beliefs are threatened, we tend to feel as if we are being attacked. This often leads to arguments and strong negative feelings towards those who disagree with us or call our ideas and beliefs stupid.

Therefore, many of us tend to avoid talking about God, religion, politics and other high-energy subjects. When we talk about these things, it helps us to develop our core beliefs, which influence the results we get out of life. The problem is that we need to develop our communication skills and develop emotional control so that we can talk about these subjects and learn from each other.

However, it is more comfortable and less threatening to talk about things that are superficial or that do not make a real difference. Although it is good to spend some time on these types of subjects, it seems that most people spend too much time avoiding conversations that require insight and thought. As a result, the things that are not important become important.

Thoughts, beliefs and ideas have their own energy. They attract and are attracted to similar thoughts or related thoughts. They come together like cells in our bodies to form belief systems and mindsets. They generate emotions that move us. They are like birds of a feather. They connect to each other like pieces of a puzzle. Then, we use them to help us understand the world and see the big picture.

Just as there are worlds within worlds, there are thoughts inside of thoughts and beliefs inside of beliefs. The process can be compared to an egg or a seed. In time, an egg can grow into a whole chicken or a seed into a whole tree or even a human being, depending on what type of egg or seed it is. The same principle can be applied to beliefs, thoughts and ideas. This process is better illustrated in the lyrics of a song by George Clinton (The Funkadelics) called "Good Thoughts, Bad Thoughts":

> Travel like a king.
> Listen to the inner voice.
> A higher wisdom is at work for you.
> Conquering the stumbling blocks comes easier
>   when the conqueror is in tune with the
>   infinite.
> Every ending is a new beginning.
> Life is an endless unfoldment.

Why We Shouldn't Call Our Ancestors Slaves

Change your mind, and you change your
relation to time.

You can find the answer.

The solution lies within the problem.

The answer is in every question.

Dig it?

An attitude is all you need to rise and walk
away.

Inspire yourself.

Your life is yours.

It fits you like your skin.

The oak sleeps in the acorn.

The giant sequoia tree sleeps in its tiny seed.

The bird waits in the egg.

God waits for his unfoldment in man.

Fly on, children.

Play on.

You gravitate to that which you secretly love
most.

You meet in life the exact reproduction of your
own thoughts.

There is no chance, coincidence or accident in a
world ruled by law and divine order.

You rise as high as your dominant aspiration.

You descend to the level of your lowest concept
of yourself.

Free your mind and your ass will follow.

PRINCIPLES & ISSUES

The infinite intelligence within you knows the answers.

Its nature is to respond to your thoughts.

Be careful of the thought-seeds you plant in the garden of your mind.

For, seeds grow after their kind.

Play on, children.

Every thought felt as true or allowed to be accepted as true by your conscious mind take roots in your subconscious, blossoms sooner or later into an act, and bears its own fruit.

Good thoughts bring forth good fruit.

Bullshit thoughts rot your meat.

Think right, and you can fly.

The kingdom of heaven is within.

Free your mind and your ass will follow.

Play on children.

Sing on lady.

This message can also be applied to the word slave. Inside this word or belief are related beliefs and thoughts. The belief that our ancestors were slaves is a bad seed. If we accept it as true, we can only get bad results. We learned that it was a bad word the first time we heard it. However, we did not understand the full negativity of it because it was in the form of a seed. As we shall see by close examination, this is a very serious concept with deep implications.

Principles of Action

Common thoughts and beliefs will produce **common actions** under similar circumstances. In turn, **common actions** will produce **common results** in a common environment. If a thought receives enough energy, it will turn into a related action. The universal laws of cause and effect govern everything in this world including our thoughts and actions which will produce specific results.

We live by the laws of cause and effect every minute of every day. We depend upon them. Nature and technology are manifestations of these laws. When we put our key in the lock of our door, we expect it to unlock. If the lock does not turn, then either the lock or the key has been damaged, or we are using the wrong key in the wrong lock. The law of when we do the right thing we get the right result is not base on intention but on the laws of cause and effect.

If I try to help my friend and he or she stabs me in the back, I may have done the right thing in trying to help; but, obviously, my friend was not trustworthy. I may have ignored the signals my friend was giving off before I tried to help. I did the right thing in trying to help, but I did the wrong thing in trying to help that particular person.

In Black communities all across America, we see similar patterns of culture, thought, belief and action. We see very similar styles in fashion, music, dance and language. We see it on the East Coast, in the Midwest, on the West Coast, in the North and the South. Therefore, we see the same results. Drug abuse, dysfunctional families, educational problems, crime and poverty are pandemic in every Black community across the country. Is it a coincidence or cause and effect?

If what you did, did not benefit you, then what you did was what someone else wanted you to do.

--Rue Dog

Who is benefiting from these un-natural problems? We must realize that common results come from a common cause or causes. If our actions are not producing the results we want, we must look at the thoughts and beliefs that are producing the actions. Where are they coming from?

The formula, therefore, is that common beliefs and thoughts produce common actions that produce specific results in a common environment every time. And, one of the most damaging beliefs that we have about ourselves is that we are the descendents of a people who were slaves to White people.

The Issues

The Intent of Slavery

The intent of slavery was to make Black people the **permanent underclass** in American society. The process of slavery cut us off from our mental and spiritual roots. This process makes people mentally and spiritually weak, which makes people easily controlled.

The aim of slavery is to get us to act like slaves. When this happens, it results in the loss of self-esteem and identity. When people have low or negative esteem and lose their identity, they lose their purpose and aim in life. This makes it hard for people to think clearly. It tends to confuse thought processes; and, this makes it easier for people to be manipulated and for self-destructive behavior to follow.

Since all human action begins with thought, mind control was necessary in order for slavery to produce the desired results. In the process, **African culture and customs had to be removed**. In continuing that process, the Euro-centric education systems give us very little information about our African heritage, history and cultures. And, what little we do get is manipulated to conform to the Euro-centric point of view.

PRINCIPLES & ISSUES

In the attempt to control the minds and spirits of Black African people, the oppressors knew that if they could get us to forget our history, deny our ancestors and our culture(s) that we would be more susceptible to their influence. If you want to kill a weed, you do it at its roots. Cutting us off from our ancestors and culture(s) has the same effect.

Why would our oppressors teach us the truth about our ancestry and history? They want us to forget about what they did to us. The school teachers are not the oppressors. They are only teaching what they were taught to teach. However, what they teach and how it is taught influences us to avoid wanting to learn about slavery and our African heritage.

When we were first brought here under slavery, the school system, the church, and the government promoted the thought that Black people were not human or less than human. They attempted to prove, with pseudo-science, that Black people were inferior to White people and that we were God's rejects deserving of inhuman treatment.

The picture that most of us have been educated to believe is that before slavery we lived like uncivilized savages in the jungles of Africa. We are taught that we were sold into slavery by our own kings and rulers. We are taught that in slavery our efforts to revolt or run away were almost always foiled by our own people.

Why We Shouldn't Call Our Ancestors Slaves

They propagandized the thought that if God did not want us to be in this situation we would not be in it. This idea is related to the idea that GOD made us inferior. I believe that God allowed it because we allowed it. I believe what happened was part of our learning process as a people. If we learn, we grow. If we do not learn, we die. The lesson is that the position we are in today is what happens to a people when they abandon the forms to which they have become accustomed. It is the lesson of what happens to a people when they lose their proper connection to their God and their true identity. (see The Warnings.)

Because of the messages of inferiority, to this very day, some Black people are still trying to prove that we are just as human and as capable as White people are.

The effects of slavery, like anything else, must be supported to be sustained. Otherwise, a natural healing will occur. The effects of slavery are supported by the thoughts and beliefs that were forced on us when our original cultures were replaced by European thoughts and beliefs. Some of us believe that we are still in slavery. Some of us believe that we will never get out of slavery. The goals of slavery are to keep us ignorant, unaware, and from using our minds effectively. The goal of slavery is to get us to give up and feel hopeless and defeated.

PRINCIPLES & ISSUES

Because of this, we must make a conscious effort to develop a greater love for ourselves as a people and for each other. This will naturally happen when we begin to educate ourselves about ourselves from outside the box of the Euro-centric educational systems. **The belief that our ancestors were slaves and that we are the descendants of slaves helps to sustain the affects of slavery and negative self-concepts.**

Why We Believe Our Ancestors Were Slaves

Maybe we believe it because we look at our history through the eyes of the people who captured, tortured, and then educated us. Maybe we believe it because almost everyone else believes it. Is it because every time we see a documentary or a movie about slavery (Black history) we see Black African people submitting to inhuman conditions like "slaves?" Is it because they say it over and over, "the slaves", "the slaves", "the slaves?" They seem to run it in the ground.

Maybe we believe it because we have problems dealing with that part of our history. For many of us, the images and thoughts of slavery are very painful because we naturally tend to identify with our ancestors. The pain of it automatically prompts us to avoid looking at the subject of our slavery. And, in avoiding it, we have not taken a deeper look at this issue. We have thrown the baby out with the dirty wash water. **The overall point of this book is to**

Why We Shouldn't Call Our Ancestors Slaves

disassociate ourselves from the word slave and not from our ancestors.

When Alex Haley's mini-series "Roots" came on TV in the late 70's, the masses of Black people were very eager to learn about our history during slavery. We thought we were going to learn the truth about slavery. In addition, we were starved for social recognition as a people. We thought that Roots would be something good for us to watch.

The series ran everyday for one week, and it seemed that everyone I knew was highly motivated to watch it. Almost every well-known Black actor was in it. It was an epic event. When it was over, almost everyone believed that, that was the way it was. We had seen enough.

Roots and all other movies about slavery have mixed falsehood and truth into one picture. They depict Black people in an inferior status to White people. They imply that most of us had accepted our fate and that only a few individuals fought back, if any. Therefore, we believe that our ancestors and fore-parents were slaves. But, why should we expect those who have a Euro-centric point of view to tell us the truth about our history? And, why should we accept what they say at face value without question?

The Reverse Psychology

How many times have we heard that we should be proud of our history? How can we be proud of being slaves? How can we be proud of being savages and being a backward people in Africa? How can we be proud of something of which we have little knowledge? This is a contradiction in logic. If we cannot take pride in being slaves, how can we take pride in being the descendants of slaves?

We tell our children to be proud of our history and then treat it as if it began in America under the despotism of White people. As a result, only a relatively few Black people have an interest in studying anything that relates to the origin and cultures of Black people. In effect, it is a form of self-rejection.

Believing that our ancestors were slaves allows us to believe that we are now free when the opposite may be more correct. If we believe we are free, we will see no need to make an effort to get free. Having rights to do particular things is not the same as being free. Prisoners have rights. Martin Luther King recognized the fact that we are not free in his 1963 *"I Have A Dream" speech*, when he said *"...But one hundred years later, the Negro still is not free."*[3] If we are not free, then what does freedom mean? What would it mean if we were free?

Being free means that we are free to be ourselves. In order to be ourselves, we must understand our true identity as a people and as individuals. In order to understand our true identity, we must understand where we came from, our history and our cultures.

Why We Shouldn't Call Our Ancestors Slaves

The reverse psychology is that it looks like "they" are telling us to do one thing; but, what is taught prompts us to do the opposite. It looks like we are being encouraged to study our own history, then it is treated as if it is irrelevant by giving us very little of it. And, what little we do get is distorted. What we do get does not encourage us to learn more about African people. Our education has not motivated us to do the things that help us to develop our communities and families or to have much hope for our future.

Correcting the Error

Correcting the error of calling the ancestors of Black Africans born in America slaves could start a domino effect allowing us to see and correct other negative perceptions of Black people. It could be the tipping point to correcting the excessive problems that plague Black communities across America. Sometimes small changes can make big differences. However, this is not a trivial or insignificant issue.

The idea of correcting the error of calling our ancestors "slaves" clearly goes against the grain of what we have been taught to believe about Black history in America. For some, it is like rocking the boat because this belief serves as the foundation for many other trusted beliefs. For some, it is upsetting because it contradicts what many of us have already accepted to be true.

PRINCIPLES & ISSUES

If we are going to change the negative conditions that plague our families and communities **we must re-educate ourselves** with information that leads us to have positive self-esteem, which will produce actions that heal Black communities and the individuals in them.

We must make a conscious effort to develop love and admiration for ourselves as a people and our ancestors through our philosophies, history, religions and customs as others have done for themselves. This does not require the falsification of information, only an honest and truthful look at our history and cultures. And, we have already begun this process.

The Reasons:

This book presents many good reasons why we should **not** call our ancestors or fore-parents slaves. Some of the main reasons are as follows:

- The definition does not fit.
- The word slave is a bogus word.
- This belief has a negative effect on the psyche and spirit of Black people.
- It is a form of blasphemy, which is a sin against our creation.
- It leads us to abandon the form(s) to which we had become accustomed. It leads us to turn away from studying our history and our cultures, which prevents us from developing a positive and loving

understanding of who we are.

- It promotes mental disorders among African Americans by promoting avoidance of our natural and true identity.

The underlying factors behind racism and inferiority complexes are fear and ignorance. Are we choosing to live our lives in ignorance and fear? What do you think White people would do if Black people finally got it together? How would it affect this country if equity was achieved? What would White people do? Would Black people seek revenge if we had the power? Is it better for Black people to stay in our place? When Barack Obama was running for president of the United States, these questions rose to the surface, but they were not fully addressed.

Those who seek equality for all people must realize that we cannot change the minds of those who are racist. They must change their own minds. We can influence them to change their minds, but we cannot do it for them. Therefore, if a change of mind is required, it must be of our own minds first.

UNDERSTANDING THE DEFINITIONS

Mis-education in its foundation is the cultivation of an alien identity. When people are taught that they are somebody who they are not, then this forms the basis of being mis-educated.[4]

--Na'im Akbar,
Know Thy Self

In order to understand *why we should not call our ancestors slaves*, we must start with **clear definitions** of the words **"slave"** and **"slavery."** Once we have this understanding, we can begin to look at the effect of applying the word **slave** to our ancestors and indirectly to ourselves. This will open the door so that we can effectively begin to correct the negative effects that slavery has had on us.

This book began when I was writing an article for an African American newspaper about slavery. I wanted to get a clear definition of the word slave for accuracy. As I read the definition, it hit me. The definition did not fit the actions of the people we call slaves -- our ancestors. After that, I looked up the word slave in every dictionary I came across. In the process, I also looked up the word "nigger" and had a similar experience.

What is the difference between a slave, a prisoner or a captive? In discussions on the subject, I have noticed that when most people use the word slave they are not using the dictionary's definition. The word slave has become a buzz word, and for different people it may mean different things. But, whatever the interpretation or meaning, it is still a negative word.

For a common understanding and clarity of thought, let us look at the dictionary's definition of the word slave and then see if the definition fits our ancestors. As we study the word slave, we can see that there is a difference between the words slave and slavery. **Slavery** is a system or an environment and the **slave** is the intended result or the product of slavery. Therefore, it is possible that a person could live under slavery and not be a slave.

The Definition (Slave)

The oldest dictionary I could find in the library was the *American Dictionary of the English Language* by Noah Webster, LL.D. Published in Springfield, MA by G. & C. (1867):

UNDERSTANDING THE DEFINITION

> Slave, n...1. A person who is held in bondage to another; one who is **wholly subject** to the will of another; one who has **no freedom of action**, but whose personal service is **wholly under the control of another**.
>
> 2. One who has lost the power of resistance; or one who surrenders himself to any power whatever..." (emphasis added)

Written one hundred and twelve years later, the following definition is taken from the Webster's New Twentieth Century Dictionary, Unabridged Second Edition (1979):

> slave... derived from the word 'slav' which was first applied to captives of Slavic origin in southeastern Europe.
>
> 1) A bond servant **divested of all freedom** and personal rights; a human being who is **owned** by and **wholly subject to the will of another**, as by capture, purchase, or birth.
>
> 2) One who has **lost the power of resistance**, or one who **surrenders** himself to any power whatever; as a slave to passion, lust, ambition, etc. (emphasis added)

The Connotative Meaning (Slave)

According to the definition, one cannot just be a slave. If a person is a slave, he or she must be a slave to something. The word slave also defines the dominant character of a person. **Such a person is not the product of natural development, but is man-made and artificial.** When we talk about Black people being slaves, we are saying that we (our ancestors) had totally surrendered and given up our rights to be human. And, when we talk about "the slaves," it is understood that we are talking about Black people being slaves to White people.

What type of person would a slave be? Who would give up their right to be human? What would it mean to actually be a slave according to the definition? In this context, it means that **the slave would not be able to resist the will of the master.** The slave would not even want to resist the master's will because the master would not want the slave to want to resist. The slave wants what the master wants for the master even if it is to the detriment of the slave. According to the definition, the slave is **wholly subject** to the will of the master.

The slave is one whose mind, will power and nature are <u>totally</u> possessed by one of a different mindset, will and nature. This means mind control. In order for this to happen, the slave's beliefs and thoughts must be the same as the master's thoughts and beliefs. When this happens, the slave speaks and acts as the master wants.

Accordingly, the slave makes his enemy's God his or her God. A slave would be like a zombie with no sense of self. In short, a slave would be a living contradiction to his or her own soul. In the end, the slave will self-destruct when he or she is no longer useful to the master.

Word History (Slave)

The *Henry Holt Encyclopedia of WORD and PHRASE ORIGINS* (1990) gives us a historical understanding of the word slave:

> Slave; Slav. The word slave has nothing to do with Athens in the Periclean Age, when there were twice as many people in bondage as free, or with the "African trade" that created four centuries of suffering. Slave came into the language long after the former and long before the latter inhumanity, deriving from the name of a tribe living in what is now Poland and other areas of Eastern Europe.

This being the case, then what does the current use of the word slave relate to? Why did the spelling change? Did the word have the same meaning when it changed as it does now? What did it mean before it changed? The *Henry Holt*

Why We Shouldn't Call Our Ancestors Slaves

Encyclopedia of WORD and PHRASE ORIGINS goes on to say:

> The name of these people meant "noble or illustrious" in their own tongue, but in about 6 A.D. they were conquered by German tribes from the west and forced to serve their conquerors or sold into bondage to the Romans. The Romans called them Sclavus, which became the Medieval Latin sclavus, "a Slav captive," this term of contempt applied to any bondsman or servile person. Sclavus became esclave in French and came into English as sclave, retaining the c until about the **16th century (which is the 1500s), when slave was first used.** The word Slav, for the race of people in Eastern Europe, comes from the same source, the proud "noble" tribe whose name underwent a complete metamorphosis. (emphasis added)

The Henry Holt Encyclopedia of WORD and PHRASE ORIGINS agrees with The American Heritage® Dictionary of the English Language, 4th Edition (2000) Word History which says:

> ..The word slave first appears in English around 1290, spelled Sclave. The spelling is based on Old French esclave ...The spelling

UNDERSTANDING THE DEFINITION

of English slave, closer to its original Slavic
form, first appears in English in 1538...

From Sclave and Slav to Slave

The word slave is supposed to have evolved from the
words Sclave and Slav. If the word slave evolved from
these words, the meaning did not transfer. Sclave or Slav,
as we have seen, is the name of captured Slavic tribes that
meant noble in their language. Therefore, the only
relationship that the word slave has with Sclave or Slav is
in the sound and the letters used to spell the words, **not in
the meaning**. Considering this, we can conclude that the
words Sclave and Slav were reformed to fit a particular
condition that had not existed before the African Holocaust
(Maafa) known as the Atlantic Slave Trade.

A Unique Word and Situation (slavery)

The word slavery (not slave) is a unique word that
was developed for a unique situation. It was developed to
fit a specific situation that had not existed prior to it.
Historians say that by the time the **African Holocaust
(Maafa)** began, almost *two thirds of the world's population
was already in some form of servitude or bondage*,
especially in Europe and Asia. Surely, they had words to
describe those situations.

Why We Shouldn't Call Our Ancestors Slaves

Accordingly, you would not use the word ice when you mean water. Cultures that have never seen snow have no word for snow. **Since slavery was a form of bondage that had never existed before, neither did the words slavery or slave.** Therefore, the word "s-l-a-v-e-r-y" did not come into existence until around 1530 according to *The American Heritage ® Dictionary of the English Language*, 4th Edition (2000) Word History. The "Atlantic slave trade" started at about the same time (the late 1400's). Is it coincidence?

Kenneth M. Stampp, author of *The Peculiar Institution* (1956), called it a peculiar institution **because "slavery" was a system of captivity that was different from any before it.** The uniqueness of the African Holocaust (Maafa) is directly related to the development of the words slavery and slave. Nathan Glazer points out that this form of captivity did not exist prior to our captivity by the Europeans. In Stanley M. Elkins' book, *Slavery*, in the introduction, Glazer writes:

> The slave could not, by law, be taught to read or write; he could not practice any religion without the permission of his master, and could never meet with his fellows, for religious or any other purposes, except in the presence of a white; and finally, if a master wished to free him, every legal obstacle was used to thwart such

action. This was not what slavery meant in the ancient world, in medieval and early modern Europe, or in Brazil and the West Indies.[5]

Slave and slavery were words that were made up to describe their intentions and to show that this was a different type or form of captivity and servitude. The definitions for bond-servant, prisoner of war, captive, hostage, and chattel had already existed before the words slave and slavery. Although they used these words to define what they meant by the word "slave" they do not have the same exact meaning. A new word was needed because the definitions of the other forms of servitude were not quite adequate.

The Difference (Slavery)

Slavery, the capture and trade of African people, which began in the 1400s, in many ways was different from the forms of servitude or bondage that existed before it. Whereas, **the prisoner, the captive, the bond servant and the hostage had some rights;** under slavery the Black African people would have none. **The process and intention define the word.** This is what made it necessary to come up with new words and spellings (slavery and slave) to fit the situation.

Why We Shouldn't Call Our Ancestors Slaves

The first part of the process was the capture. It put the mind of the captured in a state of shock and confusion, which was nature's way of protecting them for what was to come. It was the same type of shock that people have when they experience sudden physical trauma. The symptoms can be confusion, numbness and a drop in blood pressure. Sometimes, people go weak and fall into unconsciousness.

After that, there was the transition period which started with the long walk and the waiting in the prisons on the shores of West Africa. At this point, fear of the unknown would take over. Then, there was the trip across the Atlantic cramped in boats like sardines for about **six to eight weeks**. Millions died in the process.

The next part of the process was the seasoning camps in the Caribbean where the **brainwashing** and **"spirit breaking"** took place. After the camps, they had to get on the boats again and were transport to the United States and other parts of the Americas. After all of that, they ended up in a world that for them was like **Bizarro world** -- a land that was anti-Black, anti-African and that did not make sense logically or culturally speaking.

The Cultural Transplant (Slavery)

This was not an infusion of a belief system, it was a cultural transplant. The end goal of slavery was to gain as much control of Black people as possible and make money for as little cost as possible. Therefore, a mind (cultural) transplant was necessary. This transplant was a process that was supposed to make the African's **will** the same as the European American's will. It meant removing the African way of thinking and replacing it with the European American way of thinking. It was the equivalent of taking out the chicken's mind and replacing it with a duck's mind.

This process was methodical, relatively swift, very brutal, and based on what Europeans knew about human nature. We did not give up our African culture(s) because European culture was better. This change was forced on us. Black people were severely punished for practicing any African customs.

Therefore, most parents did not pass on what they knew about their original culture(s) in order to protect the children. This was the process that separated us from our African culture and religions. This process was continued and sustained by every American institution up through the days of Jim Crow. And the residual effects are still with us to this day.

In conjunction with being punished for practicing African customs, getting caught learning how to read, write and practice Christianity would bring humiliation, severe punishment and oftentimes death. The government, the churches, the schools and businesses supported this practice. As a result, our greatest thinkers were set on convincing White people that we were human beings. Can you imagine living in a world that does not consider you to be a human being?

This created a great void in the spirit and minds of Africans in America. In time, this void was filled when they began to let us into their schools and churches, which they had denied us access to until the end of the Jim Crow era. As we were being **digested** into their systems during the desegregation days, we did not understand the affect that it would have on us.

Before the Trans Atlantic Slave Trade, most people who were forced into servitude looked like the people that captured them. Their cultures were more similar than different. This is because natural barriers kept people in the same general regions. This was not the case with the European invasion of Africa. At that time, the African and European ways of life were about as opposite as black and white.

No other people have experienced **all** of the parts of this type of captivity. All these processes added together are what make the difference. These differences are what made it necessary to come up with new words to fit the situation. Along with the dictionary's definition, all the above define the real meanings of the words **slavery and slave**.

The Adjusted Definition (Slave)

Why We Shouldn't Call Our Fore Parents Slaves was first published in 1993. Before that, the definition of "slave" had virtually gone unchanged for over 100 years. Now, dictionaries have adjusted the definition. I can only wonder if the lexicologist had been influenced by the pamphlet. Although they use different words to define the word slave, it still comes down to the same thing. The following are the main phrases used to define and re-define the word slave after 1993.

Before 1993	After 1993
Divested of all freedom	Bond servant
lost the power of resistance	Property
wholly subject to the will of another	Abjectly subservient
wholly under the control of another	A machine that depends on anther
one who surrenders himself to any power whatever	chattel To work hard

Why We Shouldn't Call Our Ancestors Slaves

Today the word slave is used loosely. It is applied to almost any captive situation, except prisoners of war. To call a prisoner of war a slave would be an insult although they acted no differently than Black people did under slavery.

Soldiers are not called slaves even though they will follow orders to the death without question.

The adjusted definitions are not that much different from the original definition. The words used to define a slave may seem more acceptable, but if we think about it, they are not. What does abjectly subservient mean? What is chattel? I encouraged people to look up these words and compare the definitions with older dictionaries.

Confusion in the Language

I know you believe you understand what you think I said; but I am not sure you realize that what you heard is not what I meant.

–Unknown

The ability to communicate has put human beings over all other animals. It is man's most important survival skill. Also, there is a relationship between having clear

UNDERSTANDING THE DEFINITION

definitions and clear thinking. Therefore, in our conversations, it is important that we have a common understanding of the words that we are using. We need to make sure that we understand each other. We should be especially clear in our understanding of the words that are important to us. As we talk to each other, we should identify the key words and make sure we mean the same thing.

Confusion and misunderstanding in the language is the beginning of division and conflict in any family, group or society. And, **a house divided cannot stand.** Language and good communication begins with a common understanding of the words we use. For example, I heard a young man identify himself as a **gangster**. I asked him what the word gangster meant. He said that a gangster was someone who protects his family and who has good principles related to his friends and society. His definition had nothing to do with criminal activity.

The same principle applies to the use of the word slave. When Black and White scholars, historians and most other people use the word slave they are not using the dictionary's (original) definition. When the word slave is applied to conditions and situations that are different than those for which the word slave was developed, it distorts the true meaning of the words slavery and slave. And, in doing so, it undermines our understanding of the problems that plague our communities to this very day.

Why We Shouldn't Call Our Ancestors Slaves

According to Kenneth M. Stampp, Nathan Glazer and many others, "slavery" was a form of captivity and servitude that had not existed before the African Maafa (holocaust). Therefore, applying the word slavery to earlier and even present day forms of captivity and servitude is like calling water ice. Although ice is made of water, they are not the same.

WHY WE SHOULDN'T CALL OUR ANCESTORS SLAVES

Africans in America should never be ashamed of the indignities that our ancestors were forced to endure during enslavement. We should never refer to them as slaves, for they were human beings who were enslaved by others of a subhuman nature.[6]

--Anthony T. Browder
Survival Strategies, 13 Steps to Freedom

There is more to slavery than just forcing someone to work. All of us have to work for a living. Does that make us slaves? The word "slave" also has implied meanings that are not in the dictionary. Slavery means mind control from a foreign or outside source. The slave is one whose mind, will and nature are **totally** possessed by a person or people of a different mindsets, will and nature.

To be divested of **"all freedom"** means to take away that which makes people human. If we believe that we are descendants of slaves, we will see things and act according to our belief. Therefore, we must **know** that our ancestors were not slaves because knowing is greater than believing.

Reason I - The Definition Does Not Fit

To paraphrase Johnny Cochran; If the definition don't' fit, we must acquit. There are two reasons why the definition does not fit: 1) it is a bogus word and 2) because of our steadfast **resistance to slavery**.

It is a Bogus Word (Slave)

One key concept that makes the word slave bogus is found in the Declaration of Independence termed as **"unalienable rights."** It refers to the nature of human beings and our God given rights.

The Declaration of Independence

We hold these truths to be self-evident, that all men are created equal, that they are endowed by their Creator with **certain unalienable Rights**, that among these are Life, Liberty and the pursuit of Happiness...

Therefore, all human beings have **unalienable rights**. What does self-evident mean? What is a self-evident truth? Self-evident means you should be able to see it for yourself. The only way not to see it is if one has been blinded. The Declaration is saying that you should already know and understand this truth. And, if you do not see it, they are not going to explain it to you.

What are unalienable rights? They are God given rights that no human being can take away from another. They cannot be given away. They cannot be accidently or unknowingly lost. Could the people who wrote the Declaration of Independence not have known the meaning of the words "unalienable rights?"

It is impossible to be a slave or to make someone a slave, as defined by the dictionary, because it is impossible to take away unalienable rights. It is impossible to make someone **wholly subject** to the will of another and to **divest a person of all freedom** and **personal rights.**

Just as no one is totally devoid of freedom, no one is totally free as long as we must live by rules and regulations.

However, to argue the point, it is possible to limit the choices that a person can make by manipulating their environment. And, it is possible to get someone to do something that they do not want to do, especially if you threaten them with death. It is possible to trick and deceive people into doing things that are not good for them to do. It is possible to manipulate people by lying and distorting the truth if you can get them to believe it. Even if all this happened, this would not make a person a slave. In short, no matter what situation people are placed in, they still have unalienable rights.

When they came up with these new words, they made a mistake because their intentions were in error. The new and adjusted definitions of the word slave are proof that it was a bogus word when they first made it up. If not, then why change it? No human being can own another human being. By definition, the word slave is no more real than Santa Claus and the Boogeyman. As long as people are in pursuit of Life, Liberty, and Happiness, they could never be slaves. Therefore, "slave" is a bogus word and we should not apply it to our ancestors.

Resistance, a Battle of Wills

Do you believe Black people were docile under slavery? To call us slaves is to say or imply how we acted under slavery. One of the key phrases in the definition of the word slave is **"lost power to resist."** We have been taught that while the oppressors were saying, "Give me liberty or give me death" we were submitting to slavery without any type of note worthy resistance.

Nat Turner, Denmark Vesey, Ida B. Wells, Sojourner Truth, Harriet Tubman and Fredrick Douglas were only the tip-of-the-tip of the iceberg of resistance. To this day, the story of our resistance has been suppressed, grossly under told, and not recognized as it should be. It has been watered down to conform to the belief that we were slaves.

Especially during the days of antebellum slavery, the plantation and farm owners did not want us to know about the resistance (especially the violent resistance) that was happening on other plantations and farms. They tried to keep us from knowing because they did not want it to spread. And, they particularly did not want us to see their fear.

However, plantation and farm owners needed to know what Africans were doing on other plantations because it helped them in predicting what could happen on their own plantation or farm. Therefore, this kind of news was of vital interest to all farmers and plantation owners. They had to tell it, but they needed to keep us from knowing. Maybe, that is one more reason why they did not want us to learn how to read. You know it had to be front page news: **"Africans Go Wild on Plantation Killing Everybody."**

Under slavery, our ancestors acted no different than we would have acted under those conditions. Because we have been told over and over that they were docile under

Why We Shouldn't Call Our Ancestors Slaves

slavery, it has made it difficult for us to identify to them. However, the truth, according to John Hope Franklin, Lerone Bennett, Jr. and many others is that, **resistance could be found wherever the institution of slavery existed.** This is a very different picture than what most of us have been taught in the public school system or on TV.

The more we resisted slavery, the more the oppressors felt that it was necessary to make tougher laws and inflict greater punishment. However, their reaction to our resistance generated more resistance.

Because of the pressure and a will to be free, in one way or another, every Black person at that time was involved in some form of resistance against slavery.

Of course, there were many forms of resistance and our genius showed when it came to dealing with slavery. John Hope Franklin in From *"Slavery to Freedom: A History of Negro Americans,"* (1980) writes:

> Resistance could be found wherever the institution of slavery existed, and Negro slavery in the United States was no exception... (pg. 150) Self-mutilation and suicide were popular forms of resistance to slavery... Slaves fresh from Africa

committed suicide in great numbers... (pg. 151) Sometimes slave mothers killed their own children to prevent them from growing up in slavery... (pg. 152)

This may sound like self-destructive behavior. But, is it? What shall a person give in exchange for his or her soul? As pointed out by Mr. Franklin, self-mutilation was a popular form of resistance. He goes on to say:

Much more disturbing to the South were the numerous instances of slaves doing violence to the master class... (pg. 152) The times that overseers and masters were killed by slaves in the woods or fields were exceedingly numerous, as the careful reading of almost any Southern newspaper will reveal...(pg. 152) The practice of running away became so widespread that every state sought to strengthen its patrol and other safeguards, but to little avail.. Revolts or conspiracies to revolt persisted down to 1865. They began with the institution and did not end until slavery was abolished.[7]

Does this sound like a people who did not have the power to resist? Does it sound like a people who were totally controlled by another? Lerone Bennett, Jr., in his book, *"Before The Mayflower,"* also writes about what was written during that time:

> "In an instant," a writer said, "twelve hundred coffee and two hundred sugar plantations were in flames; the buildings, the machinery, the farm-houses, were reduced to ashes; and the unfortunate proprietors were hunted down, murdered or thrown into the flames, by the infuriated Negroes.".. (pg. 114) The slave smiled; yes. But, he also cut throats, burned down houses and conceived plots to kill every white person within reach. **This happened so often that many whites weakened under the strain.** Some died of heart failure. Some went insane. "These insurrections," a Virginian wrote during a period of panic, "have alarmed my wife so as really to endanger her health and I have not slept without anxiety in three months.[8]

The Effects of Our Resistance

Negrophobia: Back then, the African people generated so much fear that it became a definable term: Negrophobia. Initially, this fear was based on our reaction to slavery. And, this phobia still exists in some White people to this very day. **Fear and ignorance are the underlying drives of racism** in America today.

The history books clearly show that President Lincoln and the **abolitionists** did not identify with or have much compassion for the African people. Their education systems, the churches, the schools and their businesses clearly reflected their philosophies and beliefs about Black people. If not, Jim Crow and the KKK would have had no soil to grow in. Then, there would have been no need for the Civil Rights Movement and demonstrations in the 1960s and 1970s.

Slavery had become a mental and physical health hazard to America. On the mental side, Congress was locked up with debates over slavery. As a result, in 1836, they passed the **Gag Rule**, which threatened the "freedom of speech" for all citizens by barring discussions and petitions about slavery in Congress. If you can do it over slavery, then what would be next? This was the question in the back of their minds. As a result, politicians who had retired came out of the woodwork with outrage. The Gag Rule threw this country into a tizzy and brought it one step closer to the Civil War.

If not for our resistance to slavery and their fear of our retaliation, particularly our violent resistance, the government would not have been motivated to change what had made it a world power. They did not come up with the Emancipation Proclamation out of the kindness of their hearts. After they got over the Gag Rule fiasco, not long before the Civil War, there was talk in the government and in politics of ending slavery (at least changing its structure). Just as it was about to happen, **states began to secede from the Union**.

As the states began to secede from the Union, President Lincoln declared, "A house divided cannot stand." As with the concept of many gangs, "blood in blood out," the United States would not be a divided house. The **Civil War** followed and lasted for four years and ended in 1865. This war is noted as the bloodiest war America has ever fought. They did not fight a Civil War because they had to protect our interest or to rescue Black people.

You do not try to fix something that is not broken. If it is not broken, then you can only improve on it. Was slavery broken or did they just improve on it or both? **Because slavery and our resistance to it had become a health hazard to America, the system had to be changed.** It was our resistance that caused them to come up with the talk of ending slavery, the Gag Rule, the secession of states from the Union, the Civil War and the Emancipation Proclamation.

Further proof that they would have kept us in slavery if they could have can be seen in the fact that life for the African hostages did not change that much after the Emancipation Proclamation. It was slavery by another name. It is clear that even after they ended slavery they still did not let us go. Plus, most of us didn't have any where to go.

They had to change the look and condition of slavery because of our resistance to slavery. Clearly, our resistance to slavery proves that we were not slaves.

The state of resistance to slavery by Black people is the main reason why the definition of the word slave does not apply to our ancestors. The truth is that Black people were not "wholly under the control of another," and that we had not "lost the power to resist." The words "no freedom of action", and "owned by another," do not apply to our ancestors. Therefore, the word slave does not apply.

Considering the laws and attitudes of society back in those days, it must have taken a great deal of courage to fight the oppressors, to attack the "master" directly. Even those who ran away knew that if they were recaptured it would mean humiliation, torture, and maybe death. Black people must have been very brave. Therefore, we should not call our Ancestors slaves.

Even the new adjusted definitions do not apply because no human being can own another human being. And, we were not their chattel, property or abjectly subservient. Therefore, the word slave does not apply.

Reason II - Effect on Mind and Esteem

Effect on the Mind

The mind is often compared to a computer. If we programmed a computer with **incorrect information**, the answer(s) that the computer gives will be correct **according to the information it is using**. If the computer has no hardware damage, using the information it has, it will produce the same answer(s) every time.

In the same way, people can justify their actions even if they know their actions will bring negative results. People may act as if they want to go to prison by following all the necessary steps to get there; but when they get there, they only want to get out. Repeat offenders may wonder why they keep doing the same things over and over and as a result suffer every time. <u>The problem is not with their ability to think</u>, but with the information that is being used.

As a result, some people have come to believe that something is naturally wrong with them. They may say to their self, "What is wrong with me?" They may see themselves as being innately evil, stupid, dumb, crazy or all of the above. They tend to believe that others know them better than they know their own selves. Such people have accepted the idea, thought or belief that they should not "trust in their own understanding."

Or, they may believe that they are afflicted by a mental disease or disorder known as compulsive behavior. Compulsive behavior is the result of **repetitive** thinking. Repetitive thinking is the brain-computer using the same information over and over again. Since it has no other information to act on, it uses what it has.

We can tell if the information we are using is good or bad by the results we get from our actions. Good knowledge will produce good results. It produces the actions that produce the results that will benefit us.

If we follow the directions on the cake box to the letter and the cake turns out bad, something must be wrong with the instructions.

Because the attack on our self-concept has been so long and wide spread, some of us have been convinced that the reason the cake continues to turn out bad is because something is wrong with us or that we are not trying hard enough. So, we try harder, doing the same things over and over getting the same negative results every time.

A Common Core Belief

A core belief is information that serves as the foundation or support for many other beliefs. A core belief is often learned at an early age. For example, if we believe that darkness is evil and light is good, then it follows that

Why We Shouldn't Call Our Ancestors Slaves

anything associated with darkness may be considered evil, at least to some degree; and anything light could be considered as good. Our belief in GOD is a core concept because it influences our understanding of the world and our personal experiences.

The belief that our ancestors were slaves is a **core belief** and a **common belief** on which other negative beliefs about Black people have been founded and supported. Beliefs about our ancestors are core beliefs because they are central to our beliefs about our **origins** and we acquire them at an early age.

If we can believe that we were slaves, we can also believe that we lived like savages in Africa, that we sold ourselves into slavery, and that what happened to us was our fault and that we deserved it. And, a few of us have even come to believe that slavery was good for us.

The doll experiments by Kenneth and Mamie Clark (1940's-1954) and Kari Davis, "A Girl Like Me" (2005) in which African American children were asked questions related to how they felt about themselves and Black and White people are clear examples that we acquire negative core beliefs about Black people at an early age. The belief that our ancestors were slaves supports these feelings and beliefs.

In turn, these beliefs support more negative beliefs and misunderstandings about why some Black people do what we do. In the end, the subliminal message is that something is naturally wrong with Black people and that our condition and situation will never change for the better.

The fact that it is a **common belief** gives it even more power to affect the esteem of Black people, to influence how we see each other. The power of any belief or thought is dramatically increased when many people believe it or think it rather than a few. Because it is a common belief and a core belief, it permeates every part of our society right down to our personal relationships.

The Good Tree and the Bad Tree

The parable of the good tree and the bad tree reflects the **logical order** or process of how thoughts and core beliefs work in the mind. Aware of it or not, our minds will follow this logic. This parable by Jesus illustrates the law of how we relate our beliefs about our ancestors to ourselves.

MATTHEW 7:

16) You will know them by their fruits. Do men gather grapes from thorn bushes or figs from thistles? 17) Even so, every good tree bears good fruit, but a bad tree bears bad fruit. 18) A good tree cannot bear bad fruit, nor can a bad tree bear good fruit. 19) Every tree that does not bear good fruit is cut down

and thrown into the fire. 20) Therefore by
their fruits you will know them.

This is a spiritual law and a law of the mind as well
as a scientific and physical law. This law works backwards
and forwards. Metaphorically speaking, if the tree is bad,
we know it will produce bad fruit. In the same way, *good
thoughts produce good actions, which produce good
results.* If we get bad results from our actions, we know it
is because of bad or incorrect thoughts.

Our ancestors are the people from
whom we descended. If the fruit does
not fall far from the tree, then what are
we saying about ourselves when we call
our ancestors slaves? If we call them
slaves, even if we are not aware of it, by
logical process and by association, we
will subconsciously apply certain basic
traits about slaves to ourselves.

Calling our ancestors slaves promotes the idea of
inferiority of the race in relation to White people. When
low or negative self-esteem is established, a person
becomes more susceptible to psychological oppression,
mental illness, manipulation and defeat. It makes us more
susceptible to the propaganda and the mis-education from a
culture that has a long history of oppressing Black African
people. As a result, to this very day, some Black people are

still trying to prove that they are just as talented and intelligent as White people.

When people subconsciously believe that they are bad or evil or inferior, they will justify and value those qualities and feelings because they "innately have the **Drum Major Instinct**." They need to feel good about themselves and this generates the need to justify their thoughts and actions.

They are correct and justified according to the information they are using. So, to them bad is good and wrong is right. This thought process is reflected in our language and our music. As a result, to this day, many of us have no problem calling ourselves and each other **pimps, players, hustlers, gangsters, thugs, hoes, bitches,** etc. And, if we see ourselves and each other as being these types of people, we will act accordingly.

This perspective has led us to have a general lack of respect for each other and ourselves. We try to play it off by putting it in the form of a joke or by pretending that we are just having fun, but the words are still cruel and harsh. We call it cracking or throwing lugs. As I hear us talking to each other, I hear attitudes in constant attack and beat down mode. It seems that as soon as we find ourselves in a hole, our friends tend to want to beat us down even more. They always want to bring up our mistakes and make us see that our intentions are not honorable.

Why We Shouldn't Call Our Ancestors Slaves

In turn, we will pass these perspectives to our children and treat them accordingly. Believing that we are the descendants of slaves coupled with the negative images from the propaganda machine and the psychological trauma that has been passed on from one generation to the next has left too many parents with very little room for compassion and understanding for our own children. We can see it in our actions and attitudes toward our children. Why do so many of us believe that it is necessary to curse, swear, and beat our children? In short, too many of our children are being treated like slaves by their own parents. Why? Because of our negative subconscious beliefs about who we are and our origins.

How many times have we heard Black people say, "We are our own worst enemy?" We are not killing and hating each other over shoes, colors and control of the hood. These are superficial reasons that we use when we do not know the real answers. There are deeper reasons. The crimes that we see in the news that do not make sense happen for a reason. There is a self-destructive thought process behind them. These problems occur because of how we view ourselves and each other. It is a matter of self-esteem.

The Drum Major Instinct

To understand further the effect of calling our ancestors slaves and the power of self-esteem, it is necessary to understand what Dr. Martin Luther King called the "Drum Major Instinct" (DMI). **Instinct is intrinsic knowledge** that we have at birth. It is **not** the kind of knowledge that you learn in school. It is the kind that tells you how to breathe and eat. It is the kind of information that tells the body and the brain how to work together. It is the kind of knowledge that is the driving force of life.

The following are excerpts from Dr. King's speech, "The Drum Major Instinct," given at the Ebenezer Baptist Church, Atlanta, Georgia on Feb 4, 1968:

> We all want to be important, to surpass others, to achieve distinction, to lead the parade. Alfred Adler, the great psycho-analyst, contends that this is the dominant impulse. Sigmund Freud used to contend that sex was the dominant impulse, and Adler came with a new argument saying that this quest for recognition, this desire for attention, this desire for distinction is the basic impulse, the basic drive of human life, this drum major instinct.

> And you know, we begin early to ask life to put us first. Our first cry as a baby was a bid for attention. And, all through childhood the drum major impulse or instinct is a **major**

obsession. Children ask life to grant them first place. **They are a little bundle of ego.** And, they have innately the drum major impulse or the drum major instinct.

According to Dr. King, we are born with the Drum Major Instinct. In fact, we have it before we are born. It is directly related to the ego and self-esteem. It is the knowledge that is in our **Life Force.** It is directly related our **unalienable rights and the pursuit of happiness.** Dr. King goes on to say:

Now in adult life, we still have it... **We like to do something good.** And you know, we like to be praised for it... Everybody likes it, as a matter of fact... Nobody is unhappy when they are praised, even if they know they don't deserve it and even if they don't believe it.

We can see the Drum Major principle in all human activity. We can see it in individuals as well as in whole societies. It dominates the business and the advertisement industry. Everyone says that what they are selling is the best. Every society says that their way of life is the best. They always say that their actions are for the good cause. Furthermore, Dr. King says:

There comes a time that **the drum major instinct can become destructive...** if this instinct is not harnessed, it becomes a very dangerous, pernicious instinct... if it isn't harnessed, it causes one's personality to become distorted...[9]

Not only must the Drum Major Instinct (DMI) be harnessed, **it must also be nourished**. It must be controlled and fed. It must be fed a healthy diet. If it is not fed a healthy diet, it will cause the same problems as not being "harnessed." It will cause the mind to produce destructive thoughts and conflict.

Believing that our ancestors were slaves tends to distort and kill the DMI in us. It is a negative core belief about our origins which provides the foundation for negative self-esteem issues and identifications.

Self-Esteem Controls Our Actions

Self-esteem is not just an emotion. It is a set of thoughts, beliefs and values that produce an emotion or feeling. Low self-esteem leads to under achievement. Negative self-esteem leads to behaviors that divide us and that produce self-destructive behaviors. Most of the time, it is impulsive. It is behavior that comes from a set of thoughts that have been planted in the subconscious mind. When we see the actions that are produced by these thoughts, we tend call them senseless.

We act according to who we think we are. Who we think we are is our self-concept. Self-concept and self-image are directly related to each other and can mean the same thing. Maxwell Maltz in his book *The New Psycho-Cybernetics* writes about the power of self-image:

> The self-image then controls what you can and cannot accomplish, what is difficult or easy for you, even how others respond to you just as certainly and scientifically as a thermostat controls the temperature in your home.
>
> Specifically, all your actions, feelings, behavior, even your abilities, are always consistent with the self-image. Note the word: always. In short, **you will "act like" the sort of person you conceive yourself to be**. More important, you literally cannot act otherwise, in spite of all you conscious efforts or willpower. (This is why trying to achieve something difficult with teeth gritted is a losing battle. Willpower is not the answer. Self-image management is.)[10]

Self-Esteem and Survival

> Self-esteem is essential for psychological survival... You have the capacity to define who you are and then decide if you like that identity or not. But, when you reject parts of yourself, you greatly damage the psycho-

logical structures that literally keep you alive.[11]

--McKay and Fanning,
Self-Esteem

Because of the propaganda that has its roots in slavery and has persisted through the 70s until this day, many of us have fallen under its hypnotic power. Black America has been inundated with thoughts, beliefs and actions that produce low self-esteem and negative self-esteem. Again, this effect is reflected in the high rates of homicide, Black on Black violence, divorce and single parent families, incarnation, lack of education, depression, self-destructive behavior and even physical illness.

Mental Disorders

When the DMI is not properly feed and when self-esteem is low and/or negative it leads to mental disorders. All dysfunctional and self-destructive thinking and behavior is related low and/or negative esteem. When this is added to the imbedded racism in the society and the trauma from slavery that has been passed from one generation to the next, it promotes the mental disorders that Dr. Akbar describes in his book, Akbar - Papers In African Psychology, in the chapter on *Mental Disorders of African Americans* (1980).[12] In this chapter, he gives an excellent definition of **mental health** and he also lists the disorders that are pandemic in African Americans which are supported by pervasive mental and physical oppression. These disorders are:

- The Alien Self Disorder
- The Anti-self Disorder
- The Self Destructive Disorders
- Organic Disorders

How many times have we heard Black people say, "We are our own worst enemy?" We are not killing and hating each other over shoes, colors and control of the hood. These are superficial reasons that we use when we do not know the real answers. There are deeper reasons. The crimes that we see in the news that do not make sense happen for a reason. There is a self-destructive thought process behind them. These problems occur because of how we view ourselves and each other. It is a matter of esteem and self-esteem.

In turn, we will pass these perspectives and attitudes on to our children and treat them accordingly. We can see it in our actions and attitudes toward our children. Why do so many of us believe that it is necessary to curse, swear and hit our children? In short, too many of our children are being treated like slaves by their own parents. Why? Because of our negative subconscious beliefs about who we are and our origins.

Most likely, parents who abuse their children were abused when they were children. Child abuse is not a natural act. Therefore, I believe that epidemic rates of child abuse in the Black community can be traced back to the slavery days when it was the general practice to abuse Black people. All Black people suffered some form of mental and physical abuse under slavery; and, it has only been passed down from one generation to the next. In addition, nothing was done to help us heal the trauma from that experience. There have been programs to help us adjust to our situation, but not to heal the trauma.

Therefore, parents should not use anger to correct their children. They should not expect their children to function on an adult level. They should treat their children as they would want to be treated if they were children. They should respect their children.

Children who are abused by their parents should seek help and endure until help comes. Parents need to understand that what they give to their children the children will most likely give back to them in return. The bottom line is that all human life is sacred and should be respected.

Reason III - Abandonment of Form

Because of the negativity behind the word slave, believing that our ancestors were slaves tends to prevent us from identifying with them. When we lose that connection, we lose our connection to that from which we came. When people are mentally and spiritually cut off from their source(s), they suffer from spiritual illnesses. It is similar to having our food or air cut off. As McKay and Fanning have pointed out, *"When you reject parts of yourself, you greatly damage the psychological structures that literally keep you alive."*

What does it mean to abandon something? To abandon means that we are giving up something or leaving something without intending to get it back or return to it. This is not what our ancestors intended when they were forced to give up the cultures and religions of their fathers.

What is form? I use the word **form** as it is used in the Declaration of Independence when it said, *"the Forms to which they are accustomed."* As used here, forms could mean religion, culture, nature or Law. It could mean all of the above. Form is the pattern that makes the chicken a chicken and the duck a duck. Each has its own form.

Abandonment of form or ignoring our African and African American history and cultures is the result of the DMI in us reacting to incorrect and negative information about our ancestors, cultures and history. How can we identify with a people who would watch their children being abused and sold, who suffered all types of indignities at the hand of the oppressor and then willingly served that oppressor? The DMI in us will not allow it because it wants to identify with that which is good and avoid that which is negative. Therefore, too many of us have little interest in and respect for our history, our cultures, and even ourselves.

We should not call our ancestors slaves because it leads to **abandonment of form** which is **a violation of natural law and a violation of human nature.** The cause or fault of this violation does not matter. It cannot be justified. Whatever the reason, the result is the same. If someone shot you with a gun by accident or on purpose, it would not change the affect of the wound.

One of the primary objectives of slavery was to separate Black people from our original and natural cultures, from our natural ways of thinking and living. Why was it necessary for them to make African culture and customs illegal? The answer is because they knew it would make us more vulnerable to what they were trying to accomplish which was to make Black African people the permanent underclass in Euro-American culture. The "Founding Fathers" understood this principle when they adopted the Declaration of Independence on July 4th, 1776 and said, "Mankind is more disposed to suffer than to abolish the forms to which they have become accustomed."

Abandonment of form is a twofold problem: 1) of being separated from the forms to which we had become accustomed and 2) of taking on the forms of a people who are as different from us as black is from white. This problem is clearly illustrated in the allegory of the chicken and the duck.

The Chicken and the Duck Allegory

The chicken having been raised in a duck's environment by ducks grew up thinking just like a duck. The chicken had the same values and beliefs as the ducks. It saw the world through duck eyes. When the chicken looked at its own reflection, he only saw himself as being a different kind of duck. The chicken did not think that he was strange because he saw other chickens that thought and acted just like he did. And, because the chicken thought like a duck, it acted like a duck.

Eventually, the time came for the ducks to go into the water. The chicken followed. However, chicken feathers are not water proof. So, when he entered the water, he drowned while all the ducks watched in amazement wondering why the chicken did not float.

Even though the chicken did not know how to act like a chicken, the fact is that it was still a chicken. The same applies to Black people in America. Where a person is born and raised does not change what that person is. Just because the lion is born in the zoo that does not change the fact that it is still a lion. However, being born in a zoo will influence what it thinks and knows and how it acts.

The chicken, although he did not know it, was suffering from an identity problem. Even though the chicken and the duck are both birds, the chicken's actions were in direct contradiction with its own nature. The conflict that permeates Black communities across this country is enhanced by the mis-match of culture to people. European culture was not formed or designed to meet the mental and spiritual needs of Black African people.

The natural process of identification can be seen whenever a group of people move into a foreign culture or environment. Such people are inclined to take at least some of the basic elements of their cultures with them. Every major city in America has ethnic groups who have formed their own communities. When you go into these communities, it is like visiting a foreign country. In these communities, they speak their native tongue and practice the traditions of their homeland. They form these communities because it is necessary for their spiritual, mental and physical growth and development.

African people jump into life acting like Europeans. Then, we wonder why life does not work for us in the same way it does for Europeans.

The Warnings

Of all the affects of slavery, the most devastating was the **cultural transplant** because it put us in violation of natural and supernatural law(s) as they relate to our identity. It was the first step in the process of separating us from the forms to which we had become accustomed. And, it was sustained long past the Emancipation Proclamation. It has caused us to think like Europeans and to see our African cultures as repulsive. This problem is at the root of our disproportionate suffering. Calling our ancestors slaves promotes and helps to sustain these violations. It works to keep us from being ourselves.

Of course, this is not true for all Black African Americans. In fact, more and more of us are beginning to educate ourselves about our true identity, our original cultures, and our history from our perspective. **We are beginning to come around like our ancestors knew we would.**

Because many of us believe that we are all the same under the skin, we have not analyzed the problems of the Black African American correctly. There are similarities and differences underneath the skin. Just as we can understand the analogy of the chicken and the duck, other credible sources have recognized the principles of identity. The Declaration of Independence, a paper on which this country has built its foundation, acknowledges the principles on which human identity stands.

The Declaration of Independence

...Prudence, indeed, will dictate that Governments long established should not be changed for light and transient causes; and accordingly all experience has shown, that Mankind are more disposed to suffer, while Evils are sufferable, than to right themselves by abolishing the Forms to which they are Accustomed.

In this case, the word "Governments" can mean any process that guides or governs the actions of people such as religion or culture. Another way to translate the Declaration of Independence is: *Solid judgment, wisdom, and experience, beyond doubt, have proven that life styles that have been established over many generations should not be changed for reasons that are minor or short lived. All that we have read, seen, and experienced has proven that human beings will suffer more than what is natural or survivable when they abandon the styles of life through which they have evolved.*

The principles of abandonment of form are also recognized in a book, *Natural Magic*, by Francoise Strachan (1974):

> ...trouble always begins when one approaches a magical system that is basically not in harmony with one's own true nature. Contacting the wrong powers only weakens the delicate structures of the

aura, and eventually the person can become adversely affected.

Religions are magical systems and cultures are systems that have magic in them. From the same book, *Natural Magic,* the following is a caption under a picture of a White female missionary sitting on a chair surrounded by a number of bare breasted Black African women who are sitting on the ground. The caption reads:

> A missionary at work amongst her pupils... Sometimes the introduction of a completely different religion can remove the subject from the protection of the mores of their own culture.[13]

The warning against abandonment of form can also be found in the KJV of the Bible:

Deuteronomy 13

> :6) If your brother, the son of your mother, your son or your daughter, the wife of your bosom, or your friend who is as your own soul, secretly entices you saying, 'let us go and serve other gods, which you have not known, neither you nor your father. :7) Of the gods of the people which are all around you, near to you or far off from you, from one end of the earth to the other end of the earth, :8) you shall not consent to him or

listen to him, nor shall your eye pity him,
nor shall you spare him or conceal him; :9)
but you shall surely kill him; your hand shall
be first against him to put him to death, and
afterward the hand of all the people...

Jane Roberts, in her Seth book, *The Nature of Personality Reality*, describes another aspect of this law. She explains how each culture and ethnic group has its own set of standards, values and beliefs that dictate to them what is positive and negative, good and bad, desirable and not desirable. She calls it the "state of grace." At one point, she applies this rule to Black people who are accepting a Euro-centric belief system as their own. She says:

A black man who accepts the same system is
indeed in difficulty. If he happens to be a
poor black man, he is in double jeopardy.[14]

Spiritual Possession

Some people have laughed at me for this one. That is because they interpret spirit possession from a Hollywood perspective. In psychology, they call it identification, which means taking on the characteristics of another person. The following quote is taken from a psychology book titled "Psychology."

Through identification, we take on the
characteristics of someone else in order to
share in that person's triumphs and avoid

feelings of personal incompetence. Identification is considered a form of defensive coping because it enables people to resolve conflicts vicariously. [15]

The cultural transplant that was forced on Africans during slavery may also be viewed as a form of spiritual possession or forced identification on a mass level. John S. Mbiti, in his book, *African Religions and Philosophy*, 2nd ed, (1989) gives us an explanation of the affects of spiritual possession:

> But on the whole, spirit possessions, especially unsolicited ones, result in bad effects. They may cause severe torment on the possessed person; the spirit may drive him away from his home so that he lives in the forests; (in our case the streets) it may cause him to jump into the fire and get himself burnt, to torture his body with sharp instruments, or even to do harm to other people. During the height of spiritual possession, the individual in effect loses his own personality and acts in the context of the "personality" of the spirit possessing him. The possessed person becomes restless, may fail to sleep properly, and if the possession last a long period it results in

damage to health. Women are more prone to spirit possession than men...[16]

Although the term spiritual possession my sound superstitious, the description fits the situation. It provides a good description that explains the epidemic problems that we are experiencing in Black African American communities across the country.

The Transplant Phenomenon

Just as there are correlations between the physical world and the spiritual world, we can see a correlation between human organ transplants and the **cultural transplant** that was forced on us during slavery. In comparison, it is not difficult to see how the affects can be transposed to Black African American people as well.

When an organ is transplanted, the body will attempt to reject the organ because it sees it as a foreign element even though it means death to the whole body. The transplanted organ is producing internal conflict. Therefore, special drugs must be administered to get the body to accept the foreign organ.

This is just another example in nature that can help us understand what is happening to us as a people. We are experiencing what I call **cultural rejection;** and, in the process of trying to cope with the transplanted culture, drug and alcohol abuse have become epidemic in Black communities across the country.

Why We Shouldn't Call Our Ancestors Slaves

The Dynamics

The above warnings are based on the universal laws of identity, self-esteem and our true nature. The problem has two sides. One side is that of being disconnected from our natural forms and spirits. The other side is that of identifying with or taking on the forms and spirits of others.

All of us have heard the expression; body, mind, and spirit. All three were meant to function together as one to help support our unalienable rights. When all three parts are working together, we have harmony, peace, love and success. When this happens, we will see the results in our communities, families and personal lives.

Calling our Ancestors slaves and believing that African cultures are wrong and inferior to European cultures leads to the abandonment of our natural life styles and values. When we abandon our natural life styles and values, we create a mental and spiritual void. Voids must be filled. Because of this, we have been compelled to take on the life styles and values of other people.

Human culture is as necessary as breathing and eating. Therefore, every human being has a **predisposition** for culture. Without culture, we would have no functional mind, no language and no order in the family and the society. In fact, we would have no society or family without it.

European culture is a product of European minds and spirits formed according to the needs of European people. African cultures are the product of African minds and spirits formed according to the needs of African people. These cultures were developed over hundreds of thousands of years by the people for the people.

Not only do we have a need for culture, we have a predisposition toward African cultures and ways of thinking. **The proof** that we have a **natural inclination toward African styled cultures** and ways of thinking can be seen in the way we practice Euro-American culture. Clearly, we see things differently. "Nobody does it like us." In general, our churches, music, dance, art forms and mannerisms are different. In many cases, even our voices sound different.

When the Europeans wrote the Declaration of Independence, they made it clear that they were not abandoning the forms to which they had become accustomed. As a result, it is not hard to see that American culture is base on European culture. In essence, American culture is an extension of European cultures. African American culture should be an extension of African cultures. In turn, we will pass on these perspectives to our children and treat them accordingly.

Believing that we are the descendants of slaves coupled with the negative images from the propaganda machine has left too many parents with little room for compassion and understanding for our children. We can see it in our actions and attitudes toward our children. Why do so many of us believe that it is necessary to curse, swear, and beat our children? In short, too many of our children are being treated like slaves by their own parents. Why? Because of the subconscious beliefs about our origins and who we are.

Being separated from the forms to which we had become accustomed is at the root of all of our excessive problems and suffering in American society. We are practicing European culture in an African way and it is not working for us. It is producing internal conflict, which is producing conflict in all areas of African American life. Calling our ancestors slaves helps to sustain this effect.

I am not saying we should go back to the way we lived before the Europeans invaded Africa. I am saying that we need to understand our own cultures and beliefs and make the proper adjustment for the society we now live in based on our own cultures, traditions, and beliefs.

Reason IV - A Form of Blasphemy

What is Blasphemy?

Blasphemy: 1) a: the act of insulting or showing contempt or lack of reverence for God b: the act of claiming the attributes of a deity 2) irreverence toward something considered sacred or inviolable 3) language expressing disrespect for God or for something sacred.

Matthew 15:4) For God said, Honor your father and your mother; He that speaks evil of father or mother, let him die the death.

--Jesus Christ

When people use the word blasphemy, they are generally referring to references made about their God. But, it also can be applied to anything that is considered to be sacred. Blasphemy is disrespect toward something that is reverent. Blasphemy against that which is or should be sacred to us has put us in conflict with ourselves, Nature, our ancestors and higher spiritual beings. Blasphemy is language that says we have abandoned our sacred forms.

If the history books called our ancestors niggers or niggas, we would be highly upset. But, what if calling our ancestors slaves was worse than calling them Niggas? Before we make a determination, let us go to the dictionary and compare the definitions. If you had to be called one, which would you chose? If we find that the word slave is worse than calling them niggers or niggas, then it would not be hard to understand how calling our ancestors slaves is a form of blasphemy.

Why We Shouldn't Call Our Ancestors Slaves

Universal Beliefs about Ancestors

Honoring or venerating the ancestors has been a universal tradition of all cultures around the world since the dawn of civilization. How is it that these civilizations have come to practice the same beliefs and traditions independent of each other? Before slavery, our ancestors had been practicing that same tradition for thousands and thousands of years. If not for slavery, we would still be doing it.

All over the world, people believed that their ancestors had the same basic needs in the spirit world as they had in the physical world. Therefore, they made symbolic or spiritual offerings for their ancestors to assist them in the spiritual world. In turn, their ancestors would assist them in the physical world. They believed that if they did not give thanks and offerings to their ancestors they would suffer great misfortune on Earth and that their ancestors would suffer in the spiritual world.

They believed that their ancestors looked out for them and their families in their daily activities. They believed that their ancestors worked to guide them in the right directions and bring them "good fortune." They believed that their ancestors mediated for them to their God(s) and other spiritual forces and vice versa.

In turn, the elderly were highly respected because they would soon enter the spiritual world and be able to assist those in the physical world. In addition to that, the elderly were highly respected because of their experience in life. They especially deserved respect if they had taken the time to educate their selves about their culture and history.

This belief is also related to honoring and being respectful to our parents, whether they are right or wrong. Our parents are the last link in the chain that connects us to Our Source. Of course, some of us may have parents that do not deserve to be honored or respected. However, two wrongs do not make a right. And, it does the children no good to act like their parents in these situations.

Spirits at Work, or is it Luck?

Is GOD a spirit? Are angels spirits? Are saints spirits? Are our ancestors spirits? Are spirits forces? Are we spirits in the flesh? As they live in the spiritual world, our ancestors want the same thing for us that any parent would want for their children. Could what we call **luck** be our ancestors working or not working for us according to our thoughts and actions?

What we call "luck" is the result of endless chains of events that cross paths and form new chains of events according to the laws of cause and effect. If we find money on the street, run into an old friend in an unlikely place or have a close call with death; we might say we were lucky. Some people prefer to use the word fortunate. Sometimes, the outcome defies the odds. One minute of time could make all the difference. Sometimes, things just turn out better than planned. Whatever the reason or cause, we can say that there were **higher forces at work.**

Our Ancestors and History are Sacred

Sacred means that something is worthy of veneration. To venerate means to honor and respect something on a high level. Our ancestors deserve veneration. Calling them slaves is doing the opposite.

The Life Force in us has been passed on from one generation to the next from the first people that God made. That life force or spirit, along with the genetics of our physical bodies, from our Creator to us is an **unbroken chain** that connects us to Our Source and you to me. If the link from Our Source to us had been broken at any time, we could not be here.

Our ancestors are part of the process that brought us into physical existence. That which brought us into existence is sacred. Our ancestors can be considered to be sacred because they are part of the process that made us. If you love something, then you would also naturally love the process that brought that thing into existence even if the process is ugly. If we love ourselves, then we should love that which brought us into existence. Our history and our ancestors are part of that process. Therefore, we should consider them to be sacred. If not sacred, they should be highly respected. The problem is that we have been mis-educated when it comes to understanding that process. So, if we are going to find the truth of the matter, we are going to have to work for it.

Our ancestors are as sacred as Jesus. Everything that Jesus has done for us, our ancestors have done for us. We know our ancestors existed. We believe that Jesus existed. Surely, our ancestors would have avoided slavery if they could have. Was it Jesus' fault that he had to die on the cross? In the KJV, Matthew 26:39, Jesus prayed to God asking not to let what was about to happen, happen. Jesus did not want to suffer or die. Was it our ancestors' fault that they had to suffer the cruelest form of captivity in the history of the world? They deserve veneration because of what they had to go through in order for us to be here.

When children ignore their parents on purpose, it is called being disrespectful. When parents see their children ignoring them, they tend to become upset. The parents still love the children, but they do not love what their children are doing. The same applies to our history and our ancestors. Therefore, not knowing our history and calling our ancestors slaves is a form of blasphemy. It is a sin because it leads to separation from that which brought us into existence. It is very similar to abandonment of form in its effect.

Why We Shouldn't Call Our Ancestors Slaves

Although it is **not intentional**, it still produces the same results as abandonment of form. However, because it is not intentional, **forgiveness is possible**. We can correct the error. But, when we break our connection to our ancestors we break our connection to our Creator as well.

Calling our ancestors slaves is a form of blasphemy because it is not true and because in the context of our history it dehumanizes and implies that our ancestors were inferior by comparison to the Europeans who project the idea that they "would rather die than accept being a "slave." And, our history clearly shows that we resisted slavery with a vengeance. Therefore, we should not call our ancestors slaves.

Honoring Our Ancestors

By logical process, when our children see the thought process behind honoring our ancestors, they will automatically have more respect for their parents and their selves. Therefore, respect for our ancestors is critical.

Honoring our ancestors is the Drum Major Instinct being applied to them. Instead of receiving, we are giving. But, when we give to them, we receive as well. There are two ways to venerate our ancestors 1) by learning about our history, cultures and religions, and 2) through ceremony, prayer and offerings. Could honoring our ancestors bring us better luck?

Did our ancestors suffer slavery for nothing? One day, we will be part of the group known as ancestors. One hundred years from now, what will our descendents think and say about us? What do we want them to think and say about us?

Learning our history, cultures and religions is one way to show honor and respect to our ancestors. We should keep in mind that our ancestry and history did not begin with slavery. It did not begin in America. It began in Africa hundreds of thousands of years before slavery and before America existed.

In Africa, Black people were the first people in the world to develop mathematics, astrology and writing. When I first heard such statements, I found them very hard to believe. But, now I strongly believe they are true. Why didn't we learn this in school?

The hundreds of pyramids that were built by people that looked just like us is proof of the great achievements of our ancestors. Even with all the knowledge of technology that Europeans have today, they still cannot figure out how we built the pyramids. Chancellor Williams explains how the knowledge was lost in his book, The Destruction of Black Civilization, Great Issues of A Race from 4500 B.C to 2000 A.D.

We show respect and pay homage to our ancestors by walking a mile in their shoes. If our ancestors could live

Why We Shouldn't Call Our Ancestors Slaves

through slavery, we could at least look at it and learn what lessons it teaches. In doing so, **we can understand what they went through so that we could be here**. They decided to endure slavery knowing that slavery would not endure. However, most of the problems of slavery are still on us to this very day. Therefore, we need to learn the lessons. Now, it is up to us to take it to the next level.

One day, we will be part of the group known as ancestors. One hundred years from now what will our descendents think and say about us? What do we want them to think and say about us?

Ceremony, Prayer and Offerings

Another way to honor our ancestors is through ceremony, which may involve prayer and offerings such as the pouring of libation. When we are celebrating the holidays, we should set aside a moment to thank our ancestors. When we celebrate the principles of Kwanzaa, we should thank our ancestors whose names we know and whose names we do not know.

When we give thanks to our ancestors, we can feel it. Our children can feel it. When our children see us giving thanks to their ancestors it can only have a positive effect. What does that do for our children's egos when they are able to honor their own ancestors and know that they were not slaves? What would it do for the DMI in them to be part of, to identify with something worth honoring? Then, they will naturally ask why we are thanking our ancestors. We can say, because we would not be here if not for them. There is no way that they can doubt or question that fact.

It is not a violation of any religious code or principle. No religion will tell us that we are in error to give thanks to our ancestors. In fact, if these religions are for us, they would encourage us to honor and pay homage to our ancestors. If we are Christian we could say, "Thank you Jesus" and give thanks to our ancestors. Who can tell us that we should not thank our ancestors at Thanksgiving dinner or at the Christmas table or at the 4th of July picnic? Who can say that we are in error to honor, respect and give thanks to our ancestors whenever the opportunity arises?

We should include them when we are giving thanks to anything. There is no special way to do it. As long as we do it, we can do it the way we want to. All of our demonstrations, marches, and sit-ins should start with honoring our ancestors. Not just asking them for what we want, but thanking them for what they have passed on to us. Through them, God gives to us. We honor them with pictures on our walls and plaques that quote their wisdom. When we display images and symbols of our African heritage, we demonstrate love and respect for ourselves and the process that brought us into physical existence.

It can only help build the self-esteem and confidence of our children, our families and even the adults. What type of message are we sending to our children when they come home and see no pictures or symbols of their African heritage? When we pay homage to our ancestors, we show love for them and ourselves. We do not honor our ancestors by calling them slaves.

Summary

If there is nothing good about being a slave, how can we be proud of being the descendants of slaves? This is one of the main reasons we do not spend much time thinking about slavery, "the slaves" and the affect slavery has had on us.

If we simply stopped calling our ancestors slaves, that alone would not heal the disproportionate suffering in our communities. However, calling our ancestors slaves has a domino effect that leads to more serious errors and problems. Calling our ancestors slaves helps to sustain the negative effects of slavery. Correcting this error starts the process that helps us see each other and ourselves in a better light, a light that leads to improving the quality of our lives. It is a necessary step toward healing the negative effects of slavery.

Therefore, we should not call our ancestors slaves because:

The definition does not fit because it is a bogus word and because of the amount of resistance to slavery by our ancestors. The more recent dictionaries have adjusted the definition by using words like; "owned by another", "one who is the property of another", "chattel" and "abjectly subservient." Even though the definition has been adjusted, Black people still should not accept the word slave being applied to our ancestors. We were not their chattel or property. The adjusted terms do not apply. Just because they said it, that does not make it true. As Amos Wilson has pointed out in *The Falsification of Afrikan Consciousness*:

> "When we permit another people to name and define, we permit another people to gain dominion and control over us."[17]

Just because a person can hold another person hostage, it does not mean that they own them. Maybe, people can own animals, but not human beings. People who believe that they can own another person need to re-think their position. For them to believe that they owned us says something about their state of mind. Just because they believe it, it does not make it so. And, our resistance to slavery clearly demonstrates that we were not **abjectly subservient**. Therefore, even the adjusted, modern day definitions of the word slave do not apply.

Calling our ancestors slaves has a **negative effect on the self-esteem** of Black people in general. We will act according to what we believe we are. It is a core belief that has a negative influence on how we see our history, our ancestors, each other and ourselves. It also interferes with our ability to think clearly because it is incorrect information that the logical mind is using to analyze the world and our place in it. It suggests inferiority and leads to certain types of psychological disorders that are particular to African Americans.

It leads to **abandonment of form**, which leads Black people to reject who we are, our true identity and to try to be who we are not. It is like the chicken trying to be a duck. Rejection of our history and culture is the result of the DMI, the ego, and the self-esteem in trying to protect itself. Abandonment of form is the result of bad information that leads to internal conflict, which we can see manifesting in our communities and families. It leads to self-destructive behavior.

It is a form of **blasphemy**, which relates to the spiritual forces that work for us and that have a strong unseen influence on the events in our daily lives. If there are higher spiritual forces that influence our lives, if they are our ancestors in the spiritual world, we should not disrespect them by calling them slaves. We should respect them by thanking them and learning about them.

IN THE END

Is It Because I'm Black?

The dark brown shades of my skin only add color to my tears. That splash against my hollow bones that rocks my soul. Looking back over my false dreams that I once knew, wondering why my dreams never came true. Chorus: Is it because I'm black? Somebody tell me what can I do... Something is holding me back. Is it because I'm black?

Syl Johnson - Is It Because I'm Black
(Twinight Records 1970)

The answer is, no. This question implies that we suffer more because we are Black. It implies that being Black, of African descent is a curse. Being Black and living in the White man's society may seem like a curse because racism and its propaganda are just as prevalent as ever and we have very little protection from them.

For our ancestors, living in America was like being in Bizarro world, like living in hell; and it is still like that for us to this day. In conjunction with the racism, the propaganda machine would have us believe that we are the problem, that there is something intrinsically wrong with us and that we should not question a culture that was built by "slavery."

Being of Black African descent is actually a blessing because it has given us a unique spirit and perception. It has allowed us to deal with a situation where others may not have done so well. Considering our history in America, the fact that we are doing as well as we are is proof of our greatness. Further proof can be seen in how well we do in sports, entertainment, in business and even in the streets. We have proven that we can hold our own when given a fair chance and even when not given a fair chance. Just think how well we will do when we overcome the problems that divide our families and communities.

When We Do the Right Thing

Into each life a little rain must fall because no one can do the right thing all the time. No one knows everything and no one can see everything. However, we are more disposed to suffer, while Evils are sufferable, because we are in violation of spiritual and mental laws of which we are not aware. People who are not aware of the laws or rules of Nature are more likely to violate them.

The situation is similar to the computer that has been programmed with incorrect information. Therefore, many of us believe that we are doing the right things and getting the wrong results. The key to our success and happiness is to understand that when we do the right things, we get the right results every time.

Every day, we watch our children fall into all kinds of TRAPS. They are falling into the same kind of traps that we fell into when we were their age. Felonies and divided families are not what we want. The only difference in the traps today is that they have been improved. We can even see it happening on reality shows like Cops, Bate Car and The First 48hrs. What we have failed to realize is that we have been educated to fall into these traps or not educated so that we will fall into the traps.

In understanding the principle of doing the right thing, we must also consider the environment in which the action takes place. A thing may be right to do in one place and wrong in another place. However, when we do the same thing, under the same conditions; we will get the same results every time. **This is the law of action.** This is why we see the same results in Black communities from one end of the country to the other.

We have been educated to work in their world and mis-educated in how to live in our own world. Therefore, the same thing that works in their world, does not necessarily work in our world and vice versa. Because of our position as a people, we must learn how to live in two different worlds.

Why We Shouldn't Call Our Ancestors Slaves

The condition of our people is a matter of a common experience, which is producing thoughts and actions that are producing results that do not benefit us collectively. As Carter G. Woodson, the founder of Black History Month, said in the preface of his book _Mis-education of the Negro,_ "Our education has made it necessary." His statement could be rephrased to say; our experience and education has made it necessary. Therefore, we must re-educate and educate ourselves.

Tell the Children

The following is an experience I had that illustrates why we need to educate our children about us. I was riding the bus on Rosa Parks' day. The front seat of the bus had a sign on it that honored Rosa Parks. Then, a lady got on the bus with about four or five children. They sat in the front next to me, so I asked the kids if they knew who Rosa Parks was. They did not know, so I asked them about Martin Luther King. The oldest boy said, "He died." I said, "Every one dies. What else did he do?" They did not know. So, I asked them, how did Martin Luther King die? One little boy said, "He got shot coming out of a bar." Then, the woman looked at me and laughed.

Even more disturbing, I was having a conversation with a few children who were middle school age. I asked them if they were being taught anything about Black people in their classes. They looked at me as if talking about Black people was a no-no. One of them said they had heard the name W. E. B. Dubois, but that was all that they knew.

Then, I asked them if they knew where Black people came from. They answered, "GOD." I rephrased my question and asked them where Black people came from when we were first brought to America. They hesitated, and then answered, "African-American." They believed that they were from "African-American" as if there was a place by that name.

We need to understand what our children are being taught about who they are and where they came from. We need to ask them questions and find out what they think about themselves and Black people in general. If our children are not learning about themselves in a positive way, they will not develop a true or real love for self and those like self. Love for self and love for GOD is a two way street. You cannot love one without loving the other.

"He who knows nothing, loves nothing. He who can do nothing understands nothing. He who understands nothing is worthless. But he who understands also loves, notices, sees ... The more knowledge is inherent in a thing, the greater the love.... Anyone who imagines that all fruits ripen at the same time as the strawberries knows nothing about grapes."[18]

— Paracelsus

Why We Shouldn't Call Our Ancestors Slaves

The fact is that he who knows nothing about self can have no love for self. Knowledge of self includes knowledge of the mind, body Nature and the Universe as well as knowledge of our cultures and history. And, because we are a part of the universe and nature, self-knowledge would include these areas as well.

Therefore, as adults, we must re-educate ourselves so that we can educate our children properly. There is no way around it. It is our **unalienable duty** to teach our own children who they are and where they came from. We cannot depend on others to teach us about us. We cannot **totally** depend on a system that has a long history of oppressing Black people to educate our children or us about us.

We do not need to be experts or professors in Black studies, African American history or African history and culture. We do not need to memorize all the dates and names. We just need to have a general, truthful understanding of our history and cultures. It is our duty to encourage our children to educate their selves about who they are and where they came from.

A list of suggested materials has been provided at the end of this book to help start the process. Libraries, bookstores and the internet can provide us with more than enough information. And, if we look and we can find information on any subject we can think of. The more we learn, the more we learn. Knowledge is power.

Teach them

Teach them the definition of the word slave. They should understand the dictionary meaning and the implied meaning. What type of a person would a slave be? According to the definition, how would a slave act? Teach them that the definition does not apply because we resisted slavery with a vengeance. We were not just runaways. We did more than follow the drinking gourd. They need to understand that we were **not** docile while they humiliated us, beat us, sold our children and killed us in the most hideous ways.

Our children need to know that we did more than just pray and runaway to the north and hope the "master" would change his evil ways. We need to know that the Government did not come up with the Emancipation because they suddenly realized that slavery was wrong. Tell them how we fought for our liberty and that it was not "given" to us out of the kindness and goodness of our captor's hearts.

They knew that their actions were cruel and inhumane when they started slavery. They did not just wake up one day and realized it was wrong. They acknowledged the fact that they understood this when they

Why We Shouldn't Call Our Ancestors Slaves

legalized it and called it a "necessary evil." However, in truth, their cruelty and dehumanization methods were not necessary.

We would be doing a great disservice to teach our children that we were helpless and totally under the control of those who ran the system of slavery. Tell them how we truly felt about our captivity and that we did not suffer slavery without emotions like hatred, anger and fear. Yes, we were all of that and we were a dangerous people under slavery.

Tell them how unstable this country became from fear of our revolts against slavery. If we can talk about how we were held in "slavery," we should be able to talk about how we fought back. Tell them how we came back to help free our fellow Africans. Tell them that we may have been held as prisoners but that no one owned us because no human being can own another human being.

Tell them that the teachers are in error to teach that Black people were slaves in America and uncivilized in Africa. Tell them that the teachers are only human beings and are only teaching what they have been taught. Find out what your children are being taught on the subject. Ask them what they know about their history. You might be surprised. We know how much we know, but how much do they know?

IN THE END

We should tell our children that **all societies and all races of people have had their holocaust and catastrophes at the hands of other people** and that slavery was ours. We should explain that just because we were in slavery it does not mean that we were slaves. We should let them know that they (we) are descendents of a great people who formed the first great civilizations, invented writing, were the first mathematicians, scientist and explorers of the world. Black African people built the Sphinx and the Pyramids. Let them know that we can return to being a great people when we learn the lessons of our history and come to a true understanding of who we are.

Some Basic Questions

There are certain things about our history that all of our children should understand. Every Black child and adult should have a positive answer and understanding to the following questions:

- What continent did Black people come from? What were the Black people like in Africa before the Europeans showed up?
- What happened after they showed up?
- What is Africa like now?
- What happened to the Africans (Black people) who were brought here under slavery?

- How many were brought here?
- Were Black people really Slaves?
- What would it mean to be a slave?

Did We Sell Ourselves into Slavery?

As we have accepted the belief that we were slaves, we have also accepted the belief that we sold ourselves into slavery. What kind of people would sell their own people into slavery? This question is critical to our self-evaluation because it speaks to what type of people we are. Some of us tend to think that if we sold ourselves into slavery that it was our fault that we had to endure slavery. It conforms to the idea that we are our own worst enemy. Therefore, we should spend some time on this question.

By the 1400's, every culture and type of people had some form of bondage or indentured servitude. Historians say that two thirds of the European population was in some form of forced bondage. At that time, their bond servants and prisoners were protected by the laws of the land and by their governments. Their systems of servitude before the African Slave Trade were far more humane than the way they conducted the African Slave Trade.

The same applied to the African systems of human bondage. Because of this, a universal standard existed. So, when Africans sold Africans, it was not their intention to trade people into **slavery** as practiced by the Europeans.

The Africans thought they were trading human beings into a humane system of servitude, not slavery. African people had no concept of **captivity** as it was practiced by the Europeans. The African people had no idea of the racism and cruelty that the Europeans had in mind. To them, it was unthinkable.

Europeans had put the entire continent of Africa into slavery. They called it colonialism. If they could do that, why would they buy us from us? How hard would it be to get us out of Africa? They were not buying; they were taking. In the end, slavery (colonialism) in Africa was just as cruel, if not worse than the New World slavery. Therefore, it would be a misnomer to say that we sold our own people into "slavery."

What Should We Call Them?

After people understand the title of this book, they naturally ask, "What should we call them?" According to their own testimony, our ancestors called themselves slaves. But, does that mean that they were slaves? I believe that they meant something different from the dictionary meaning or the connotative meaning. Nonetheless, the word slave has become a buzzword; and as we apply it to our ancestors, we need to be clear on what we mean.

Even after we understand why we should not call our ancestors slaves, some of us will still have a tendency to want to call them slaves. I think this happens because it is a core belief and we are very use to using the word slave. Ultimately, we want to use a word that acknowledges their particular <u>situation</u>. Therefore, we feel a need to replace the word slave with another word that depicts the condition we were in at that time. In order to replace the word slave, people tend to want to use the word en<u>slave</u>d.

Enslaved: It still has the word slave in it. This word tends to lean toward the idea that we were slaves. To be enslaved means or strongly implies that one was made a slave. Enslaving someone and capturing someone are very similar terms. However, we would not say **encaptured** when we mean someone was not captured but put in a similar situation. The word enslaved has a slightly different meaning than saying, "**in slavery**."

As the word slave is used in the context of American history, it has heavy racial overtones. So, when we say, "the slaves" we know we are talking about Black African people during a particular period in American history. Do we need a special word to distinguish them from us? What criteria should we use?

- where they came from
- their intentions
- their actions
- their situation
- their social status (what we use now)

- their appearance or race

There are many other words that we can use to describe our ancestor who were **prisoners in slavery.** To try to use one word to describe them and their situation does not quite do them justice. The following words can easily be substituted for the words slave and enslaved. In doing so, it would not change our understanding of what happened. In fact, it would give us a better perspective of our history and self-concept.

- African prisoners in slavery
- African prisoners of American slavery
- American Maafa captives
- Maafa freedom fighters in America
- African captives in America
- Victims of the African Holocaust

As far as this writer is concerned at this time, it really does not matter what terms we use as long as we **do not call them slaves or use terms that imply absolute submission or inferiority.** Any combination of the above terms will do. But, whatever terms we use, we should be able to identify with them.

~Peace~

Why We Shouldn't Call Our Ancestors Slaves

The Ancestor Prayer

I Thank My Ancestors

I thank my ancestors for the here and now. I know I could not be here without them. I thank my parents who are related to my ancestors. I know they have done the best that they know how.

Even though it may seem like I am in hell, my ancestors have provided a sanctuary for me and those like me. They have proven that they love me more than I love myself.

Why We Shouldn't Call Our Ancestors Slaves

SUGGESTED SOURCES

Ask, and it shall be given to you; seek, and ye shall find; knock, and it shall be opened unto you: 8) For every one that asketh receiveth; and he that seeketh findeth; and to him that knocketh it shall be opened.

--Jesus Christ
King James, Matthew 7:7-8

Therefore, be careful what you ask for. However, if you don't ask, you will not receive. If we look for truth, we will find it eventually. Information on any of the suggested materials and great teachers can be found on the internet, in the library and book stores.

Videos:

- Daughters of the Dust (1991) Julie Dash
- Sankofa (1993) by Haile Gerima
- 500 Years Later (2005) M.K. Asante Jr
- The Lost Kingdoms of Africa (2010) by Dr. Gus Casely-Hayford, published by BBC
- Feast of All Saints, (2001) Anne Rice (book) John Wilder (teleplay)
- The Black Candle, M.K. Asante Jr.

Why We Shouldn't Call Our Ancestors Slaves

Books:

- Know Thy Self, by Na'im Akbar
- Black on Black Violence by Amos Wilson
- As A Man Thinketh by James Allen
- Destruction of Black Civilization by Chancellor Williams
- The Falsification of Afrikan Consciousness by Amos Wilson
- Survival Strategies for Africans in America by Anthony T. Browder
- African Religion and Philosophy by John S. Imbiti
- Facing Mt Kenyatta by Jomo Kenyata
- Things Fall Apart, by Chinua Achebe
- Brave New World by Aldous Huxley
- Animal Farm by George Orwell
- The Nature of Personal Reality by Jane Roberts
- The Gospel of Barnabas, Published by A&B Publisher Group
- Slavery, by Stanley Elkins
- Beating Black Kids by Asadah
- Post Traumatic Slave Syndrome, by Joy DeGruy, Ph.D
- Too Young to Die by Dr. Earl E Bracy.

Great Teachers

Obviously, there are many more great teachers that should be included in this list. Our history is full of them. Keep in mind that one great teacher will lead you to others.

- Dr. Ray Hagins
- Dr. Ni'am Akbar
- Minister Louis Farrakhan
- Dr. Frances C. Welsing
- Fredrick Douglas
- Marcus Garvey
- Amos Wilson
- Carter G. Woodson
- Dr. Molefi K. Asante
- Dr. Maulana Karanga
- Dr. Leonard Jeffries
- Anthony Browder

Why We Shouldn't Call Our Ancestors Slaves

End Notes

(qop = quoted on page)

---

[1]As A Man Thinketh "Thought & Character" by James Allen, (ISBN: 0-88029-785-9, 1992) p. 2 [qop, 1]

[2]Brainwashed, Challenging the Myth of Black Inferiority by Tom Burrell, (ISBN: 978-1-4019-25925,) p. ix [qop, 4]

[3]Martin Luther King Jr. I Have A Dream, ed by James M. Washington (ISBN: 0-06-250552-1) p. 102 [qop, 25]

[4]Know Thy Self by Ni'am Akbar, (ISBN: 0935257-06-3) p. 5 [qop, 29]

[5]Slavery, A Problem in American Institutional & Intellectual Life, "Introduction" by Stanley M. Elkins, (LCCN: 59-12284, 1963) p. ix [qop, 37]

[6]Survival Strategies for Africans in America by Anthony T. Browder, (ISBN: 0-924944-10-2, 1996) p. 113 [qop, 45]

[7]From Slavery to Freedom: A history of Negro Americans Fifth Edition by John Hope Franklin, (ISBN: 0-394-32256-8, p. 150-153 [qop, 51]

[8]Before The Mayflower, A History of Black America by Lerone Bennett Jr., (ISBN: 0 14 00.7214 4, 1982) p. 114-115 [qop, 52]

End Notes

---

[9]I Have A Dream, Writings & Speeches, "Drum Major Instinct", edited by James Melvin Washington, (ISBN: 0-06-250552-1, 1986) p. 182-185 [qop, 65]

[10]The New Psycho-Cybernetics by Maxwell Maltz, MD., FICS, (ISBN: 0-7352-0275-3, 2001) p. 3 [qop, 66]

[11]Self-Esteem by McKay and Fanning, (ISBN: 1-57224-198-5, 2000) p. 1 [qop, 67]

[12]Akbar, Papers In African Psychology by Na'im Akbar Ph.D. (ISBN: 0935257101) [qop, 67]

[13]Natural Magic by Fransoise Strachan, (ISBN: 0-88486-002-7, 1974) p 85 [qop, 76]

[14]The Nature of Personality Reality, A Seth Book by Jane Roberts, (ISBN: 1-878424-06-8, 1994) p. 251 [qop, 77]

[15]Psychology, Charles G. Morris (ISBN: 0-13-734194-6, 1973) p. 615 [qop, 78]

[16]African Religions and Philosophy, 2nd ed by John S. Mbiti, , (ISBN: 0-435-89591-5) p. 80-81 [qop, 79]

[17]The Falsification of Afrikan Consciousness by Amos N. Wilson, (ISBN: 1-879164-02-7, 1993) p. 22 [qop, 93]

[18]Paracelsus, Quotable Quote, http://www.goodreads.com /quotes/show/139506 [qop, 99]

End Notes

Notes:

End Notes

Notes:

Made in the USA
Lexington, KY
23 October 2014